Great Aunt Jane's Cook and Garden Book

Great Aunt Jane's Cook and Garden Book

JANE BIRCHFIELD

J. B. Lippincott Company
Philadelphia and New York

Compilation copyright © 1976 by Jane Birchfield
All rights reserved
First edition
Printed in the United States of America

Illustrations selected from *1800 Woodcuts by Thomas Bewick and His School*, edited by Blanche Cirker, and *Handbook of Early Advertising Art*, by Clarence P. Hornung, are reprinted with permission of Dover Publications, Inc.

U.S. Library of Congress Cataloging in Publication Data

Birchfield, Jane, birth date
Great Aunt Jane's cook and garden book.
Includes index.
1. Cookery. 2. Gardening. I. Title.
TX715.B499   641.5   76-22729
ISBN-0-397-01176-8

For Jim
A good, kind man—and one most dear.
Though gentle, yet not dull; deep, yet clear.
Strong, without rage; honest, without guile,
One whom all can trust and no man fear.
You've brought the taste of goodness
To each day these forty year.
May it still be so, yet awhile—awhile.

Contents

Acknowledgments 11
About the Recipes 13

THE FIRST SEASON

JANUARY

Chili for a Snowy Day 17
The Post-Holiday Blahs 21
Sweet 'Tater Pies, Puffs, and Such 25

FEBRUARY

Biology, Birds, and Bees 32
Blackbirds, Herbs, and a Woman's Worth 37
Biscuits and Birthday Cakes 43
Foretaste of Spring 48

MARCH

Deceptive March Days 52
A Mess of Pottage and a Cottage Loaf 57
Beans, Beans, Beans 61
Sparragrass and a Good Cheese Companion 64

THE SECOND SEASON

APRIL

Everything Happens in Spring	71
Easter Ham and Eggs	73
The Dandy Dandelion	77
Good Breads	81

MAY

Of Herbs and Other Country Messes	88
The Young Gardener	90
Apples of Love and Bean Poles	93

JUNE

Gifts for the Bride	97
The Year of the Rabbit Is Right!	101
Wildflowers of Summer	104

THE THIRD SEASON

JULY

A Report from the Garden	111
Garden Raiders Are Persistent Cusses	114
A Blackberry Summer	117
Curses in the Corn Patch and Other Places	121
A Surfeit of Squash	123

AUGUST

Barricades, Beetles, Broodies, and Lazy Beans	130
Pickle Time	133
The Tyranny of Tomatoes	138

SEPTEMBER

Autumn Woods	144
Sesame or Benne	147
Girasoles or Jerusalem Artichokes	152

THE FOURTH SEASON

OCTOBER

Virginia Is for Apple Lovers	159
Of Pepo, Pompion, Punkin, Pumpkin	164
Pawpaws, 'Simmons, and Such	169

NOVEMBER

Game Plan for Feasts	174
Great Native Nuts	178
Corn, the All-American Grain	183
Thanksgiving Feast Coming Up	189

DECEMBER

Cookie Time—Christmas Is a Comin'	194
Cups That Cheer	203
Goops, Christmas KP, and a Chili Roundup	205
Of Machines, Mary Anns, and Good Gifts	211
Index	217

Acknowledgments

Much of the material in this book first appeared in the *Piedmont Virginian,* either as sometime articles or as my regular Great Aunt Jane column. Thanks be to the editor, Ray Dilley, for doing all the things a good editor does to give aid, comfort, and encouragement to a writer.

When a reader wrote and mentioned "the taste of goodness," I was curious about the expression, never having heard it before. He had first heard it used more than fifty years ago, to explain how a wonderful cook named Irma managed to make everything taste so good. The more I thought about the expression, the more it seemed to apply to a lot of things. Not just the food we cook or what we eat and drink, but what we read or write, the music we play or listen to, even what we make of our daily lives and associations with other people—all this can reflect our taste of goodness. So thanks be to Taylor Holt, Jr., for giving me the idea.

Parts of the book first appeared in a column I write for the magazine *Spur.* Thanks be to Gwen Dobson, who was the first to urge me to write more about country cooking.

A lot of readers asked me to collect the columns in a book, but it was a long-time friend and former publisher who got the project under way. After seeing some sample columns he asked for more, got them all into good hands, and gave me hope and good cheer during the period of waiting to see what, if anything, would happen. Thanks be to Victor Weybright, not just for his advice and practical help but for the many times he brightened my day or lifted my spirits with encouraging and amusing letters, an occasional old cookbook to add to my collection, and clippings of anything and everything he thought might be of interest.

Many other people have been helpful and encouraging since the Great Aunt Jane columns first appeared. Thanks be to all of them for ideas, kind comments, and contributions to the columns.

How I wish Frances, my dear friend and faithful helper, could be here today! For over twenty-five years she gave us loving-kindness and comfort in our sorrows, made the rough places smooth, and shared our joys. It still doesn't seem right, somehow, to have anything happen in our lives that she can't be a part of.

Near Ashburn Junction Jane Birchfield
March 15, 1976

About the Recipes

WHERE fairly accurate amounts, proportions, temperatures, and cooking times are important, they are included. The terms moderate, about, and so on indicate that minor adjustments can be made without altering the character and quality of a dish.

Except in a few cases I do not indicate number of servings, since an adequate serving for one person may not fill the hollow tooth of another. For the same reason, I try to avoid giving exact amounts of seasoning. Tastes differ.

There is no such thing as a "born" cook. There are people who, by their very nature, seem to enjoy food: the color, the taste, and the texture. They learn to cook by *cooking* and—probably without realizing it—by using all five senses; taste, feel, sight, smell, and, yes, sound. Only you can tell when a flavor and an aroma please you. Weather, temperature, humidity, altitude, and a number of other variables can affect certain ingredients and techniques used in cooking. To make good pastry, bread, or roll dough, you have to learn, from experience, how it should *feel*. In frying, baking, or roasting, only by sight can you tell when something is brown, but if you listen to something frying you can hear whether it is cooking too rapidly or not fast enough. (When I make jelly I never have to give it the standard tests, letting it sheet off a spoon or dropping some on a saucer to cool; I can tell by the changing size and sound of the bubbles when it is ready to jell.)

14/ About the Recipes

All of the recipes have been tested. Not scientifically, mind you, but on the many stoves in the several kitchens in which I have cooked over the years, as well as by the many good cooks—past and present—who are kith and kin and friends.

Unless otherwise specified the baking powder used is a double-acting combination type. The brand I use includes *only* calcium acid phosphate, bicarbonate of soda, and some cornstarch for filler. When you buy baking powder read the label; in fact, read the label on everything you buy and use. For each cup of flour in a recipe use 1 tsp combination-type baking powder. If you prefer to use a single-acting tartrate or phosphate type of baking powder, use twice as much, i.e., 2 tsp per cup of flour. It is very easy to mix your own single-acting baking powder but easier still to just substitute ¼ tsp soda and ½ tsp cream of tartar for each teaspoonful of single-acting baking powder called for in a recipe.

In all recipes calling for cornmeal I use the white water-ground type. In some parts of the country there is a preference for yellow cornmeal, and in some places only stone-ground white is available. Any of the three can be used. If I couldn't get the white water-ground meal, I would sure make do with what I could get—*any* cornmeal is better than none at all.

Some recipes call for using rose water as a flavoring. Someone asked if this wasn't a perfume. Well, just as a rose is a rose is a rose, rose water is rose water is rose water. For centuries it has been used to give a delicate flavor to a number of foods, especially cakes, cookies, and candies. In some countries it is used to flavor everything, and the cruet of rose water is as prevalent as the ubiquitous bottle of catsup on the American lunch counter. It is also used in a number of ways that have nothing to do with food or cooking: among others, it makes an excellent eyewash, when mixed with witch hazel it can be used as a freshener on the most delicate skin, and mixed with glycerine it makes a marvelous hand lotion.

The First Season

JANUARY
Chili for a Snowy Day

*Down comes the soft and silent snow,
White petals from the flowers that grow
In the cold atmosphere.*
      —George W. Bungay, "The Artists of the Air"

WHAT do you do on a snowy day? The first thing I did when the snow began to fall on Monday was to put a pound of pink beans on to simmer and get meat from the freezer to start thawing—the makings of a big pot of chili. Next, I put on my boots and went out to fill the bird feeders and get the mail down at the end of the lane. Then, back in the house, I settled down for what I think of as a good snow day: a day when you change your pace and do the sort of chores that will allow you to sit by a window and watch the snow fall.

If snow is something you have to scrape from the windshield and drive through cautiously to avoid smashing into a tree or another automobile, then you don't have much time to enjoy the magic and beauty of what is happening. But if you can take the time to sit and look, what a miracle happens, right before your eyes! Of course, if you haven't lost your sense of wonder, the same sort of miracles are happening all around you, every day. The late Rachel

Carson wrote a wonderful little book called *The Sense of Wonder*. I found paperback copies of it, just at the right time to give some young mothers a gift that they in turn could give to their children, for Christmas and the rest of their lives.

But back to my snow day. While the pot of chili bubbled and plopped on the stove and the old clock gently ticked away, I sat by the window and polished silver while watching the snow . . . and the birds. An equally good job would have been mending. How many people, I wonder, have a mending basket these days? In fact, I wonder how many people know what a mending basket *is*, much less what to do with it.

Today, young people sew patches on their vintage jeans just for the decorative effect. Back in the days when I sewed patches on jeans, they were decorative and amusing but they were put there to cover places that were worn or torn. Our son, Johnny B., took the prize for breaking in (or should I say breaking out of?) new britches. In no time at all he could manage to rip out the entire seat of a new pair of jeans. When asked "How come?" his stock explanation was, "The bob-wire fence reached out and grabbed me."

As I polished the silver I also thought about the young people who don't want silver, because it has to be polished. Aren't they missing something? Of course it is less time-consuming to use stainless steel and dump it in the dishwasher, but sometimes the things that require special care give special gratification. Heaven knows I'm not a fanatic about spit and polish; as a matter of fact my housekeeping is so casual as to be chaotic. But when I do get around to polishing the silver it gives me a great sense of accomplishment to see it all lined up, softly shining with the patina that comes from age and use.

All of this, in turn, makes me wonder what many people do with all the precious time they have saved by using objects that require no special care—serving "convenience" foods, using electrical appliances to do everything that

Chili for a Snowy Day / 19

once kept idle hands from the devil's work. Do they devote all that saved time to doing something useful or beautiful with their hands; are they using their minds to *think*, their eyes to *see*? I hope, but doubt, the answer is "yes." In my experience the people who save the most time do the least with it.

But enough of these snowy-day thoughts. Back to the practical, i.e., the chili. (Just for clarity I spell the pepper with an "e," the dish with an "i.") Nothing is more comforting to come home to, on a cold snowy night. Depending on my mood, and available ingredients, I make it a number of different ways. This was Monday's version.

CHILI CON CARNE. Sort and wash 1 pound of pink beans, cover with water, and cook at a slow simmer for several hours. (Did you know that beans require longer cooking in hard water? And that salt shouldn't be added until they are at least half done? You see, there's a better way to do everything, even cooking a bean.) While the beans are getting done, in another, and larger, pot cook 2 large chopped onions in a small amount of bacon drippings until soft. Add 1 pound each of good pork sausage and lean ground beef. Stir and continue to cook until the meat is crumbled and lightly browned. Add 1 T molasses (this doesn't make it sweet but rounds out the other flavors), 1 tsp dried oregano, 4 T chili powder (more can be added later if the final dish is too bland), salt (about 2 tsp for starters), and 2 quarts of canned tomatoes. Let the meat mixture simmer until it is fairly thick. About an hour before serving, add the cooked beans and juice and continue to simmer to blend all the flavors.

To go with the hot chili I made a cool, fresh FRUIT SALAD: chopped apples, celery, nuts, and grapes, with a dressing of mayonnaise thinned down a bit with buttermilk.

Then at the last minute I made a batch of HUSH PUPPIES—just water-ground cornmeal and salt (1 tsp to each cup), mixed with enough boiling water to make a stiff dough, dropped into hot deep fat by teaspoonfuls, and fried until brown. This made a meal, and a good one. And by making this quantity of chili there's enough left over to stash in the freezer for a future cold, snowy night.

Saturday morning I got an SOS: what to do with a cup of whipping cream? My suggestion was a WHIPPED CREAM CAKE, and after passing the recipe along it seemed like such a good idea I made one for us. (A lot of recipes called whipped cream cake are just any cake, dressed up with a layer or topping of whipped cream. In this one the cream goes in at the start.) Beat until stiff, but not dry, 3 egg whites and ¼ tsp salt. Shift to a large bowl and in first mixer bowl whip 1 C heavy cream until it holds a peak. Add cream to egg white and gently fold in ½ C water and 1 tsp flavoring.

Combine 2 C sifted cake flour, 1½ C sugar, and 2 tsp baking powder. Sift together 3 times and then fold into the first mixture, a spoonful or two at a time. This should make a very light, airy batter. Bake in greased 9-inch tube pan for about 45 minutes in a moderate oven (350° to 375°). When done, it should be just a light golden color. Turn out on rack. When cool, spread with a seven-minute frosting. If I flavor the cake with vanilla, then I flavor the frosting with peppermint; almond-flavored cake is good with coconut frosting.

This cake is different in that it is moist *and* light. Since commercial sour cream is more readily available than fresh, heavy sweet cream, I am going to see if I can't work out a variation using the sour cream.

A lot of things can be done with the 3 egg yolks not used in the cake, but perhaps the most elegant and easy is SABAYON. In the top of a double boiler or a bowl that can be used over a pan of boiling water mix 3 egg yolks with 6 T sugar and just a pinch of salt. Beat constantly while it cooks over the hot water (using a hand mixer or eggbeater); add 6 T wine, continuing to beat constantly until mixture thickens. (Any dessert wine can be used, but we prefer Almond Cream Marsala.) As soon as it coats the beater, pour into parfait glasses and serve immediately. It can be chilled but it is traditional to serve it warm, when it is more light and fluffy.

If you want to make a cold Sabayon that can be made ahead of time, use 3 whole eggs instead of just the yolks. Proceed as above but, when mixture is cooked, fold in 3 stiffly beaten egg whites before chilling.

The other evening, while wheezing with asthma, I was naturally interested in an item in one of my old cook-and-household-hint books promising "Certain Relief from Asthma." Didn't feel very hopeful after reading it, however: "Sufferers from asthma should get a muskrat skin and wear it over their lungs with the fur side next to the body." We have the muskrats, all right, down at the pond, but I just don't have the inclination.

In the same book there was an equally impractical suggestion for preparing truffles. It started out: "Select some fine truffles, at least two per portion. . . ." With truffles now bringing $200 per pound wholesale, who needs it?

The Post-Holiday Blahs

How weary, stale, flat, and unprofitable seem to me...
　　　　　　　　　　　—*Shakespeare,* Hamlet

MAYBE it's the letdown after the holidays, or it could be the combination of bills (bigger than you thought they would be), bank statements (smaller than you had hoped), and those food prices that continue to go up, up, and away! Whatever the reasons, few of us escape the kitchen doldrums right now. If we could just put the stove, refrigerator, and sink on "hold" for a few days, we might return to the routine with zest. Failing this, the next best

January

thing is to try something new and different or tackle some job that will provide an outlet for aggressions and frustrations. (Punching and kneading dough for home-baked bread is excellent therapy, and the end result is enjoyed by all.)

For something new, you might try concocting a series of crunchy, bite-size bits of goodness. They go with everything from cocktails and soups to that bedtime glass of milk. The basic recipe, CRUNCHY BUTTONS, starts with 1 C flour, mixed with ¼ C fresh wheat germ and 1 tsp kosher salt. Work in ½ stick of butter with fingers or blender until mixture is mealy. At this stage you make the additions that vary the flavor.

For ROSEMARY BUTTONS, add 2 T chopped, fresh rosemary leaves, 1 egg, and just enough milk to make a stiff dough. Roll out on a lightly floured board, ⅛-inch thick, cut into small rounds, about 1 inch, space on a cookie sheet, and bake until golden brown in a hot oven. (Other herbs may be used: thyme, chives, parsley, sage, etc. If dried herbs are substituted, cut down amount to 1 tsp.)

For NUTTY-CHEESE BUTTONS, add 1 C shredded sharp cheese, ¼ C grated pecans, 1 egg, and enough milk to make a stiff dough and proceed as above; for PEANUTTY BUTTONS, add ½ C chunk-style peanut butter and egg and milk as above. There are numerous other variations you might try. In a covered tin or plastic container these will all keep a long time, if you can keep them hidden.

CRUNCHY CRUST. For a different sort of crunchy texture, here's a formula for one-crust pastry, especially good for quiche or cheese pies or onion tarts. To 1½ C whole wheat pastry flour (available at health food stores) add ½ tsp salt. Work in 1 stick of butter until mixture is mealy. Add enough ice water to make stiff dough (about ¼ C). This dough is not elastic, so it cannot be completely rolled out on board. First, with rolling pin, roll out in a circle, shift to pan, and then with fingers press dough to line pan evenly and smoothly. Fill and bake as you would any pie.

For a good meal-in-a-dish, for Sunday supper, or even for an addition to an informal buffet party, HOT POTATO/FRANK SALAD is filling, interesting and different in flavor, and, even at today's prices, inexpensive. Scrub and cook 6 medium potatoes until tender. Meanwhile, cut 6 slices of bacon into thin strips and cook until crisp. Drain bacon bits and set aside. To ¼ C bacon drippings add 2 T flour, 1 T sugar, 2 tsp salt, and freshly ground pepper to taste. Blend until smooth. Add 1 C water and ⅓ C vinegar, stir, and cook over low heat until smooth. Remove from heat.

Peel and cut the cooked potatoes into ¼-inch slices and add them to the sauce, along with 1 pound of skinless frankfurters that have been cut at an angle into ¼-inch slices. Heat, stirring carefully, to coat the mixture with the sauce. Then serve on a platter surrounded with lettuce or romaine chunks and thin slices of some or all of the following: cucumber, onion, radishes, tomatoes. Sprinkle with the bacon bits and some celery seed.

Of all the good recipes in my mother's cookbook, one of the best is for a simple pudding and sauce. It took her only a matter of minutes to put it together; now it is even easier to make with an electric mixer. She would put it in the oven when dinner was served, and by dessert time it was ready to eat.

NELLIE'S PUDDING. In mixing bowl blend (at high speed) ½ C sugar, 1 egg, ½ tsp salt, and 1 heaping T butter, softened or melted. When smooth, turn speed to low and add 1 C flour that has been sifted twice with 1 tsp baking powder. When smooth (don't overstir) pour into buttered 8-inch-square cake pan and bake in moderate oven for 25 minutes.

Serve with LEMON SAUCE. To 1 T cornstarch add a small amount of cold water and stir until dissolved. Add 2 C boiling water, ¾ C sugar; cook and stir until clear. At last, add 1 T butter, some grated rind, and 1 tsp lemon juice. Serve warm on warm pudding. (It is also extremely good served on plum pudding, instead of the more usual hard sauce.)

January

If you think bread pudding is mundane, then you haven't eaten CHOCOLATE BREAD PUDDING. Cover 3½ C cubed stale bread with 3 C warm milk. Allow to soak until cool; then add 3 eggs, ½ C sugar, 4 T good cocoa, and ¼ tsp salt, all of which have been beaten together at high speed for several minutes (1½ squares chocolate, melted, may replace the cocoa). Pour into a buttered baking dish, set in a pan of hot water, and bake in 350° oven for about 45 minutes. Serve cold, topped with whipped cream.

Now that the ground is covered with snow we shouldn't forget to feed the birds. One way to see that the smaller birds get their share is to fill coconut shells with a BIRD PUDDING and hang them from tree limbs with heavy twine. In melted fat from cooked meat (including bacon) stir in some cornmeal, a handful of rolled oats, some peanut hearts or chunky peanut butter, a few raisins, and some mixed grain, cracked corn, and sunflower seeds. Cook, then pack into the coconut shells; replenish as the birds consume what you have put out. Chickadees, tufted titmice, creepers, nuthatches, downy woodpeckers, and other small birds love these puddings.

Last week I did some impulse buying, a bag of parsnips. What a good thing we've been missing when I have passed these by recently. Until I started scraping the roots I had forgotten what a fresh, lemony scent they have—more pleasing to me than most types that come in a bottle. And that flavor really woke up the taste buds.

For PEPPY PARSNIPS, scrape 1 pound parsnips and slice directly into a saucepan containing 2 C cold water mixed with 2 T vinegar. Bring to boil and simmer until slices are just tender. A few minutes before serving, heat 2 T bacon drippings in a skillet, add the drained parsnips, 1 tsp brown sugar, some shreds of hot red pepper, ¼ tsp coarse salt, and 2 T minced parsley, and toss and stir over fairly high heat until lightly browned. This amount might make four servings for picky eaters, but the two of us licked the platter clean, along with some cold roast pork.

Sweet 'Tater Pies, Puffs, and Such

Anyone who's ever had Sweet Potato Pie,
Really won't want punkin agin.
—"Sweet Potato Tin"

ONE year I cooked my way through a powerful lot of sweet potatoes. After I had planted a long row of them in the garden, someone came along and gave me another bundle of plants. Not having the strength of character it takes to toss healthy plants on the trash heap, I put them in the ground too. It was a good year. All the plants survived and thrived. Came the first light frost and time to dig, we had more sweet potatoes than I cared to contemplate.

We had them in every known shape and form, plus a few new ones I devised. Two of our daughter Tam's favorites in her brown-bag school lunch were a whole avocado, all to herself, or a cold baked sweet potato. (She got precious few avocados but a whole heck of a lot of cold potatoes.)

That same year the bees made a lot of honey and we had plenty of butter from Queen, the Jersey cow. So when the first P-TA dinner of the season asked for a contribution I sent a mammoth casserole of candied sweet potatoes. After this the word got round and I was getting requests from all over for my honey-butter 'taters. I could probably have become Sweet Potato Queen of Loudoun County, but I willingly gave up the opportunity and from then on put in fewer plants.

The sweet potato, *Ipomoea batatas*, is a member of the morning glory family. Varieties are probably native to Central America, West Indies, and East Indies, but it is grown in all warm climates, where it is an important food crop. Essential to the southern plantation economy, being productive, nutritious, and easily cultivated, it was a basic staple of diet for several months of the year, one that found equal favor whether eaten around the cabin hearth or served at the banquet table in the main house. Today, modern methods of transportation, storage, canning, and freezing make it possible to serve sweet potatoes in some form the year round and just about everywhere.

Preparation may be as simple as baking whole in the fireplace ashes or as elaborate as putting on a production that ends in flaming brandy. Sweet potatoes may be mashed, boiled, baked, fried, stuffed, used as a stuffing for other things, or served raw. They can make a satisfying and nourishing dish for the vegetarian diet, be combined with all manner of other vegetables or fruits, or be served as side dishes with many kinds of meats, especially turkey, ham, pork, chicken, and many types of game.

They're not exactly low-cal, but then they aren't all that high either—about 150 calories per medium-size potato—and they're an excellent source of vitamin A. If you have to stretch food dollars—and who doesn't?—sweet potatoes are a real help. For what you pay you get a lot of pleasing taste and nutritive value in a filling food that sticks to the ribs. Here is a sampler of recipes, starting with what could be a great breakfast with Sweet Potato Biscuits served with bacon and eggs; ending with Yams Flambé for a dramatic dessert; with all sorts of puffs, pones, pies, puddings, and main dishes for in between, even including, for the venturesome, what has to be the most soulful of all soul food, Roast Possum and Sweet 'Taters.

Many call for MASHED SWEET POTATOES. To prepare, scrub potatoes and either steam or simmer in water until tender (where possible select potatoes of same size so they will all be done at the same time). Cool slightly, so they can be handled, remove skins, mash, and use immediately or cover and store in refrigerator to be used in a day or two. Or fill containers, cover, and freeze for use somewhat later.

SWEET POTATO BISCUITS. Sift together 2 C

flour, 1 T sugar, 1 tsp salt, and ¼ tsp soda. Work in 2 T butter and 2 C mashed sweet potatoes; then add enough buttermilk to make a soft dough. Knead for about 1 minute on a lightly floured board, roll out, cut, and bake in a "quick" oven—about 15 minutes at 425°. The same dough can be used to make a crust for chicken pot pie, or you can add an egg to the basic ingredients and cut down on the amount of buttermilk.

For a hearty, leisurely, Sunday breakfast you might try SWEET POTATO PONE, served with sliced ham. This is sort of like a pudding, but not exactly. It is served hot, with the meat course, at any meal, and any left over is sliced and served cold. (Like pease porridge, some like it hot, some like it cold, but most pone-eaters will eat it any way, any time they can get it.) Beat together 2 eggs and 1 C milk and into this liquid shred 4 large, peeled, raw sweet potatoes, keeping potatoes covered with liquid to prevent darkening. Mix in ½ C each brown sugar and molasses, ½ C melted butter, grated rind of 1 lemon and 1 orange, and ½ tsp each cinnamon, nutmeg, and cloves. Turn into buttered baking dish and bake 1 hour at 325°.

SWEET POTATO PUDDING is more like a soufflé and should be served while it is hot and puffy. It is good with almost any meat but especially so with cold sliced turkey or chicken. Beat 3 egg whites until stiff, shift to another container, and in mixer bowl combine 2 C mashed sweet potato with 2 egg yolks, ½ C cream, ⅓ C brown sugar, grated rind and juice of ½ lemon, ½ tsp each cinnamon and ginger, ¼ tsp cloves, and 3 T brandy. Mix at high speed until mixture is smooth. Add salt and freshly ground pepper to taste and fold in beaten egg whites. Turn into greased baking dish and bake about 30 minutes at 350°.

I think this is good just the way it is, but if you want to get fancy you could make some additions before the egg whites are folded in, such as a small bottle of chestnuts in syrup, some coarsely chopped pecans, about ½ C white raisins, or some shredded candied ginger. If you get really carried away you could bake this in orange shells and top with marshmallows just a few minutes before the soufflé is done.

I'm not all that keen about marshmallows and other things that are super sweet so I don't make SWEET POTATO PUFFS very often, but I can be persuaded to do so. While 2 C mashed sweet potatoes are still hot, stir in about 2 T butter, ½ tsp grated nutmeg, and a pinch each of allspice and ground cloves. (You don't want to get an overwhelming spice taste.) Add a pinch of salt and let potato mixture cool; then mold it around large marshmallows to make round balls. It takes about a heaping tablespoonful to cover each marshmallow. Roll these balls in crushed cornflakes, space on a buttered baking sheet, and bake at 350° until lightly browned.

'TATER-STUFFED PEPPERS are more to my taste. Cut large sweet peppers (red or green) in half lengthwise, remove veins and seeds, blanch in boiling water for a minute or two, and place upside down on paper towels to drain. When cool, heap full of mashed sweet potato which has been seasoned with salt, freshly ground pepper, and butter. Top each one with 1 or 2 small sausage links that have been lightly browned in a skillet. Space on baking sheet and bake about 30 minutes at 325°.

Another good way to combine MASHED SWEETS AND SAUSAGE is in a casserole, starting with a layer of seasoned mashed potatoes. Top with four browned link sausages, cover with another layer of potatoes, and top with more sausage. Bake about ½ hour at 350°.

Now, about that ROAST POSSUM AND SWEET 'TATERS. First, catch your possum. To dress it, scald in a gallon of boiling water mixed with ½ C lime. Remove hair, scrape hide, cut off feet and tail, and remove entrails. If head is left on, remove eyes and ears. Cover possum with cold water, add ½ C salt, and soak for 12 hours. Drain, place possum in large kettle, cover with hot water, and cook until skin is tender. Let stand in broth until cool enough to be handled, then lay it out flat in roasting pan and surround it with slices of cooked, peeled sweet potatoes. Add some freshly ground pepper and some of the broth in which it was cooked. Roast in a 375° oven until nicely browned. Serve on a platter garnished with fresh parsley and surrounded by the 'taters.

ROAST PORK AND SWEET 'TATERS. Unless you have a passion for possum, the 'taters are just as good, or even better, cooked the same way with roast pork. Starting with loin roast of pork, score top layer of fat, sprinkle with salt and freshly ground pepper, put on 3 or 4 sprigs of fresh rosemary (about 1 tsp of the dried can be used as a substitute), and some finely snipped shreds of hot red pepper. Roast at 350° about 45 minutes or 1 hour; then add the sliced cooked sweet potatoes, turning them over in pan juices. Continue baking until roast is done; total cooking time should amount to about 35 minutes per pound of meat.

For CANDIED SWEETS that go with just about any sort of meat—or for that matter a vegetarian main dish, made with rice, bulgur, or soybeans—put sliced sweet potatoes (that have been boiled and peeled) in a shallow baking pan. Drizzle honey over the top, dot with butter, and bake in a moderate oven until glazed and brown. The amount of sweetening you add depends on the intensity of your taste for honey.

Sweet potatoes can be fried in a number of ways, all of them good, but perhaps the best is 'TATER NESTS. Peel raw sweet potatoes and cut into thin julienne strips, dropped in cold water to prevent discoloration. Drain and wrap in a towel to absorb moisture. To fry these, arrange a layer of strips in bottom half of a nest basket, hold in place with smaller section of basket, lower into hot fat, and deep-fry until crisp. (I have devised these little baskets by using two wire strainers of the same shape but with one slightly larger than the other, but it is much more satisfactory to use the little wire basket designed for this purpose—a good investment, for these crisp little cases can also be made of regular potatoes or thin slices of bread, and they taste so good when filled with creamed vegetables or meats.)

Raw sweet potatoes may also be cut into thin "chips," waffle slices, ripple strips—any way you would cut regular potatoes for deep frying. Too, partially cooked sweets can be peeled, cut into thick slices, and deep fried.

For that celebrated SWEET POTATO PIE, boil, peel, and mash 1 pound of red-flesh sweets. In mixer bowl beat 4 egg whites until stiff and shift to another bowl. Combine in mixer bowl the hot mashed potatoes, ½ C butter, 1 C brown sugar, 2 tsp cinnamon, 1 tsp nutmeg, and a pinch of salt. Blend at high speed until smooth. Turn down speed, add 4 egg yolks and the juice and grated rind of 1 lemon, and blend until smooth. Continuing at low speed, slowly add 1 C cream and 1 jigger of brandy. Finally, fold in the beaten egg whites and turn into a large pie pan lined with pastry. Bake at 400° for 10 minutes, then lower heat to 325° and continue baking until filling is set but soft. Serve with sweetened whipped cream and you really may not want punkin agin.

Is it possible to crack up over a cranky coffeepot? I don't know, but I came perilously close to finding out. For almost a year I had been "making do" with a percolator that had lost its perk. The coffee was too weak or too strong and, further, the amount of coffee I made was either too much or not enough. What a way to start the day. *Every* day.

Making the breakfast coffee was something I had done at least 14,965 times, but came the stage where I wasn't sure how much longer I could go on doing it. What I really wanted to do was to hurl that blankety-blank-blank pot through the kitchen window, run outside and stamp it to death with my feet, and then, just to make sure it was finished, strangle it with its own electric cord.

But exercising considerable restraint I turned instead to *The Cooks' Catalogue* and studied the section on coffee making and makers. After comparing the pros and cons of all systems I settled for the Toddy Coffee Maker, which operates on a different principle from any other.

Requiring only cold water and a few hours of time, it produces an essence which can be stored in refrigerator or freezer, ready any time for making as good a hot, freshly brewed coffee as we have ever tried—or the best iced coffee you could ever taste. It even *smells* like freshly brewed coffee, and the essence is always on hand to use in cooking. It is as easy and convenient to use as the brands of "instant" coffee, but there's just no comparison in the flavor and aroma. The maker comes with an attractive glass carafe (which I managed to break soon after it arrived), but any wide-mouth jar will serve the same purpose. It can be ordered directly from Toddy Products, 1206 Brooks Street, Houston, Texas, 77009.

Checking back, I see that I forgot the YAMS FLAMBÉ. Cook 3 large sweet potatoes just until tender, peel, and cut into 1-inch slices. Dredge the 'tater slices and some pineapple slices in flour, dip in milk, and coat again with flour. Fry in vegetable oil until golden brown. Drain on paper and place in one layer on a fireproof platter, putting a maraschino cherry in center of each pineapple slice. Dust with sugar, heat in a moderate oven for 5 minutes, pour heated brandy over, light with a match, and bring to the table while blazing.

When making and serving any flaming dish, use a long match and something to protect your hands when lifting the hot container. You don't want to spoil all these special effects by having a flambéed cook!

FEBRUARY
Biology, Birds, and Bees

A little learning is a dangerous thing.
—Alexander Pope, Essays

It has been quite a stretch of time since I have been around the Halls of Academe. I just plain forgot all that goes on in a science lab when I decided that would be a good place to have the herb class. The idea seemed attractive because of all that nice working space, with a small sink, water connection, and an electric outlet right at hand. But it wasn't long after we all got settled down to sniffing and tasting and comparing parsley, sage, rosemary, thyme, and the rest that I realized I must have been out of my mind when I (a) agreed to teach the course and (b) thought of holding it in the science lab.

The first indication of difficulties came when I looked over at the next table and saw what must have been a very tiny, tender, pink Pig Robinson—stretched out, stiff, waiting for the dissecting knife. Next came the strong whiffs of formaldehyde. All the aromas of cardamon, coriander, basil, and rue were no match for it. All the perfumes of Araby couldn't have wiped it out.

Trying to transcend the less pleasant aspects of the situation, I started talking about all the fascinating myth and legend connected with herbs—an attempt that wasn't entirely successful, since I started getting heavy competition from the other side of the room, where a caged (and apparently enraged) monkey started screeching and banging noisy objects about. I'll have to give the entire class full marks for making the best of a sorely trying time. Many of them had come quite a long distance for the course, all seemed to be eager and interested, and they all stuck it out.

My first order of business following that class was to arrange for some other space where we could meet for future sessions. I didn't drive a hard bargain about what would be required in the way of facilities. Running water and electric outlet? Forget it. All I wanted was a small, separate room that didn't come equipped with little pink pickled pigs, the stench of formaldehyde, and a hyperactive monkey in the corner.

Would you believe that I had earlier prepared Bean Soup with Ham for dinner? Ham! What's more, I was too tired to prepare an alternate menu. Well, at least I had enough sense to not serve pickles with it.

Another casualty of my teaching career (which I can forecast is going to be brief) is the loss of a fine pot of trailing rosemary which I took along to class as an exhibit. If it isn't dead it is at least lying there bleeding, for the sudden shock of being taken from the warm greenhouse out into the bitter cold was apparently too much. Whoever is keeping score can give me a few more marks for stupidity.

At a recent garden club get-together, what amounted to a coven of bird watchers congregated, comparing notes on what they had been putting out to provide amusement and diversion for the birds and keep them coming to the feeders—or should I say, keep the birds coming to the feeders, providing amusement and diversion for the watchers!

In any case, Anne MacLeod came up with something different: a peanut butter sandwich for the birds. She takes a large head of sunflower seed, smears it thickly with chunky peanut butter, then jams in a lot more loose sunflower seed. Though she has additional feeding stations, this "sandwich" is where the action is. This seems like such a good idea I wonder if it could be adapted. Say, take something like a corncob and suspend it from a tree limb on a string, smeared with peanut butter and then coated with grain. Might be worth trying.

This week we had a good casserole of WHITE BEANS AND LAMB. I washed 1 pound of white beans, covered them with water, and simmered them until just tender. Then in a shallow casserole I browned lamb neck chops in about 1 T bacon drippings. After lifting out the chops, I added the beans to the casserole, seasoned with salt, pepper, and some dried leaves of basil, and stirred around to mix with the pan juices. Then the browned chops were added to the beans, and they in turn were seasoned with salt, pepper, and a few leaves of rosemary. Covered and cooked slowly in a moderate oven, it made a fine meal with some Quick Crusty Bread (page 82) and a crisp salad.

It only took half the beans, so the other half went into that aforesaid BEAN SOUP WITH HAM. To the beans I had added some of the ham juice from the freezer, a pod of red pepper, some celery leaves, and onion. Shortly before serving I added 1 C chopped ham and a couple of medium potatoes that had been boiled and then mashed in the water in which they had been cooked. It was good, but it would have tasted even better if I hadn't had such a recent encounter with the little pink pickled pig.

If we're going to have a January thaw it is time to be having it. So far it just seems to be cold and colder, but I must say everything looks beautiful on these icy mornings. When the sun hits the frosty fields they look like they have been sprinkled with diamond dust. The ice-coated twigs and limbs of trees are indeed handsome, and the tiny, ice-covered multiflora rose hips shine like red jewels. And cold as it is, I find little green spears of bulbs pushing through in more protected spots. Hard and frozen it may be, but there's *something* going on down there, in the ground.

With some interest, but without being tempted to the tiniest degree, I note that the new Thompson and Morgan catalog is offering a "Complete Beginner's Outfit" for would-be beekeepers. For $195 you get a hive, what they call a "popular" smoker, a hive tool, and a bee hat and veil. For another $95 you get the bees. And $4.95 on top of that brings you the book on beekeeping with "every area spelt out in ordinary language."

According to T & M you don't need much space, the hive only requires 2 to 3 hours' attention a fortnight, "there is no heavy work and it is inheritantly suitable for women, who will find it easy and absorbing." In addition to producing all that honey to supply your family with excess to sell profitably, there is "Propolis, the sticky waxy material honey bees use to keep draughts and disease from the hive." And, in case you're not familiar with propolis, they go on to say that it prevents or cures colds, flu, sore throats, eczema, acne, bad eyes, rheumatism, and many other ailments. "Sale of excess propolis should more than cover your capital investment in the first season."

Well, we've been in and out that door and I would almost be willing to pay $300 *not* to have to keep bees! As I recall (and while it was some years ago every detail remains etched on my memory as though it happened yesterday), it was, at times, heavy work and I did not find it "inheritantly" suitable or easy. At times it *was* absorbing, in that it absorbed an undue amount of my time and attention.

With two other innocent victims, we bought six hives of bees, offered at $15 each. In the dark of night we went somewhere over in Maryland, with a trailer, to pick up the hives. All remained fairly quiet and calm until we got the hives loaded and started home. Fortunately, the bees couldn't get out of the hives, but they set up an angry buzzing that sounded like the whole load, trailer and all, was going to take off and into space. We had to stop for gasoline on the way home, and you never saw a filling station attendant get a car filled with gas so fast or look so relieved as we pulled away.

Once back here we had to go to three places and unload beehives into wheelbarrows and trundle them to appointed locations at each place, stumbling around by flashlight, expecting the hives to explode any minute.

From then on, right up to the time I noticed the last swarm and bade it godspeed, there was nothing "easy" about this venture. If you weren't scraping or smoking, adding supers, taking out frames, getting more hives to house swarms, feeding with sugar water when the honey flow was poor, or getting stung, it was a case of coping with gallons of honey that tasted downright nasty. Our bees never seemed to make honey from anything except tickseed, or if they made a better honey they ate it all themselves. We got the tickseed honey, which was a beautiful color but had a nauseating flavor.

If anybody plans to keep bees because he or she likes honey, I'll say what I said to the lady who wondered about buying a goat because she liked goat cheese. If you like honey, go find a store that sells it and *buy* some. As for the bees (or the goat), *forget it*. Be duly grateful that there are other people willing to produce honey and goat cheese for you, and divert your energies to something like crocheting antimacassars, knotting or knitting, or even making candles. *Anything* but keeping bees—or goats. In other words, to complete the opening quotation, "taste not the Pierian spring."

Blackbirds, Herbs, and a Woman's Worth

The maid was in the garden,
Hanging out the clothes,
When along came a blackbird
And pecked off her nose.

—Nursery rhyme

LAST week I declined an invitation to go down and observe the blackbirds coming in to their roost a few miles east of here. I understand it is an awe-inspiring sight, but then it is one I see about every day, twice a day, when the birds fly over going from or returning to the roost. These flocks are usually made up of red-winged and rusty blackbirds, cowbirds, grackles, and starlings, and this particular one is estimated at being around a million birds.

I don't mind a few of these different species blowing in from time to time to freeload at the feeders, and when I plant corn I always put in "one for the blackbird, one for the crow, one for the cutworm, and one to grow." But when they invade the place in huge numbers, swoop down, and nip off all the buds and blooms of miniature daffodils in a matter of seconds, my attitude becomes somewhat less permissive. Some of these little daffodils may have taken four or five years to reach blooming size after I made the cross and planted the seed. It can be discouraging to see so much work go down the drain so fast and know that an additional full year has been lost for selection and/or further hybridizing.

So far I have taken no more drastic action than to frighten them away when they begin to light in the trees. Best method for this, I've found, is to dash out the door, screaming and vigorously clanging a string of Indian temple bells. (Perhaps it is just as well that we have no near neighbors! Certainly any stray visitor who came up the lane about the time I begin this action would think I had flipped.)

As unwelcome as these red-winged blackbirds are, in the company they keep, the others that come from farther south to nest in the cattails around the pond bring joy and delight, for they're a sure sign of spring. Each year at about the same time of the month, late in the evening, I'll suddenly become aware of their lyric song coming from down at the pond. These are the male redwings that come in early to stake out nesting claims. Two weeks later, almost to the minute, the females arrive and start settling down. No matter how miserable the weather at the time, this event is a signal that winter's back is broken.

Another annual event is the arrival of a flock of robins, which usually come in on my birthday, the end of this month. Somehow there is something reassuring about being able to look out and see them in droves, prospecting for worms in the field of grass between the house and the pond. They don't hang around very long and usually are on their way north in a day or two, but as long as they arrive I have the feeling that nature is operating on schedule.

Small groups of starlings come and go throughout most of the year. On the occasions when a bunch of them are blown in by a wet and windy storm, I am inclined to wonder if they have less oil to protect their feathers than other birds. They certainly can be the *wettest*, most bedraggled, and disreputable looking. Some people haven't a good word to say for starlings (in fact, I know at least one bloody-minded bird watcher who shoots all the starlings that dare come to his elite bird feeders). I must admit they are scrappy, pushy, noisy, and quarrelsome, but they can be interesting to watch for they are also clever and adaptable. Their beaks were not designed for dealing with sunflower seed, but when push comes to shove they can learn how to eat it. And when they're sleek and dry, with iridescent feathers shining in the sun, they're not all that unhandsome. When great-niece Sassy was a little girl she used to call them rainbow birds, which is possibly the nicest thing that has ever been said about a starling. It just becomes difficult, if not impossible, to appreciate their virtues when there are too many of them congregated in the same place at the same time, competing for the same space. But that can be said for anything, including us!

All the rules of natural order get discombobulated when the space one needs is threatened by invasion or intrusion. This does not just apply to areas of habitat, countries, and cities. Each of us, whether we're aware of it or not, has a personal "space," physical and mental. The amount of space one requires varies with the individual, but whatever the boundaries it makes us uncomfortable when anyone or anything oversteps them. This basic need is the reason we all resent invasion of privacy, infringement of rights, being jostled in crowds, hemmed in by traffic, or the multitudinous other ways in which our space is invaded, even by mail and telephone.

Much of my time the past few weeks has been spent delving into the subject of herbs, trying to decide how much of what kind of information to use in my course. A lot of the legend and lore is pure fancy and in some cases very funny, but there is enough fact along with the fiction to make it seem desirable to have more objective scientific investigation of the natural curative value of plants. I don't think for a minute that putting a leaf of mugwort in your shoe will make you walk with a lighter step, nor can I give much credence to the theory that a diet of chrysanthemums can turn white hairs black, make new teeth grow in where old ones fell out, or have a man of eighty become like a boy again. But take the case of the edible burdock, gobo, which the Japanese have been eating for a thousand years. It smells good and tastes good and contains a few minerals but was thought to be of little value as a food, since it contains no vitamins or calories to speak of. Now it has been discovered that gobo is not only an excellent source of roughage or fiber and a great aid to digestion, but even more importantly it absorbs mercury compounds and is an antidote for mercury poisoning.

Don't we need more research into the curative value of those native plants that are available and abundant? Enough is already known about the curative and tonic effects of the leaves, flowers, and roots of dandelions to save a lot of money spent on weed killers and prescriptions. Furthermore, dandelion leaves taste great in a green salad or cooked with a set of greens.

Right now salad greens have soared out of sight. Even cabbage costs five or six times what it should, but even so it is a better buy than lettuce, romaine, or chicory. I make a lot of different types of cabbage salad or slaw, but the one we like best is one called LAITUE SUEDOISE; I can't remember where I first found it and can't locate it anywhere in my collection of cookbooks, but here's how it goes. To crisp, thinly shredded cabbage add some finely shredded celery, some chopped green onion (tops included) or finely minced regular onion, some chopped pimiento, coarse salt, freshly ground pepper, some whole seed of mustard and celery, a pinch of brown sugar, and a simple oil-and-vinegar dressing. This is especially good with any type of fried fish, oysters, shrimp, or crab cakes or any type of cold sliced meat.

We also like a soup that is not run-of-the-mill, TOMATO BISQUE. Combine 1 C canned tomatoes with 1 tsp sugar, a bit of bay leaf, a thin slice of onion stuck with a couple of cloves, a sprig of parsley, and 1 tsp salt. Cover and cook slowly about 15 minutes. Then either whirl this mixture in a blender or put it through a food mill and add it to 2 C milk which has been heated with ¼ C fine bread crumbs and 2 T butter. (To prevent curdling when combining tomatoes and milk, always add the tomatoes to the milk instead of the other way around.) Add freshly ground pepper and celery salt to taste and serve topped with a small glob of sour cream, dusted with paprika.

Another good hot soup for a cold day (or a hot day for that matter; the Mexicans consume quantities of it when the temperature soars) is ALBONDIGAS. Here is my version of long-time friend Midge Parker's authentic recipe, the only difference being that I use my own home-canned, herb-flavored tomatoes. In 2 T butter slowly cook until limp 2 thinly sliced onions, 1 chopped green chile (or sweet pepper), and 2 minced cloves of garlic. Add 1 tsp chili powder and 2 tsp oregano; then add 1 quart tomatoes and 2½ quarts water. Let this mixture simmer 1 hour. Meanwhile make meatballs. To 1 pound lean ground beef add the soft inner part of 4 slices of fresh white bread that has been pulled into small pieces, 2 T chopped fresh mint leaves (or 1 tsp crumbled dried mint), and 2 raw eggs. Work this all together with the hands, form meatballs the size of marbles, drop them into the simmering soup, and continue to cook on low heat for 45 minutes.

Midge says that when she first made Albondigas she followed traditional directions to add masa or cornmeal to the meatballs. They sank out of sight and never came up and had the weight of mini minié balls. Later, when she described the fiasco to her Mexican mentor and asked what to do, Señora Gomez leaned over and whispered in her ear, "Use pulled white bread." It works! The tiny little meatballs are fluffy and feather light, the way they should be. So much for authentic authenticity.

During her many periods of living in Mexico or on frequent visits, Midge learned how to make an elegant first course, EGGS IN SNOW. Peel and halve 6 hard-cooked eggs and mix the yolks with 2 T deviled ham or ham paste, 1 T each chopped parsley and prepared mustard, and about 2 T minced or grated onion. Stuff this mixture into the egg-white halves, put the halves together and mask with 1 C whipped cream, and then sprinkle with grated Parmesan cheese.

She also learned to make the SALSA (sauce) that is served over any kind of meat or fish, added to soups, or used as a dip for tortilla chips. Grind together 10 seeded green chiles, 10 tomatoes, ½ medium-size onion, 2 cloves of garlic, and some leaves of *cilantro* (fresh coriander). Mix with ½ wine glass of vinegar, 2 tsp olive oil, and salt and pepper to taste.

This past week we had some of the stuffed peppers I made and froze last fall—these were the version where I combined rice, fresh corn, onion, and tomato—and good they were. We also had a VEGETABLE CASSEROLE that I had assembled and frozen, straight from the garden. Without blanching them I filled a foil baking pan with layers of corn cut from the cob, lima beans, green beans, sliced yellow squash, green peppers, and onions. All I had to do was take the pan out of the freezer, pop it into the oven, take it out when done, and serve with a topping of grated cheese. It all tasted like fresh from the garden.

Last fall I froze peaches the easy way—by just peeling, halving, and packing two peaches to a small plastic bag and putting them into the freezer immediately. Now we are reaping that harvest. The peaches don't turn dark even though no sugar or anything else was added. We like them best served as a sort of PEACH SALAD, two peach halves on some fresh Bibb lettuce leaves, topped with a thick cream dressing, either based on blue cheese or mayonnaise. Of course they would be just as good served as a dessert with sugar and cream, or filled with ice cream. They also make good PEACHES PIQUANT, to serve with cold turkey or ham: Just separate the peach halves, fill the cavities with mincemeat or chutney, and broil until the tops are brown.

For a while there I was tempted to get myself one of those "mood" rings, just to see what it would do. Well, now I won't. One person I know got one, and as soon as she put it on it turned black and stayed that way. Not one time did it turn blue or any of the "happy" colors. Finally, after she realized the ring was adding to her feeling of depression, she tossed it out and started feeling better right away!

Another thing I have toyed with getting is a pedometer. Frequently it seems that I have to do an inordinate amount of walking to get anything done. Just found out that my friend Ruth Thomas felt the same way about her daily rounds. To find out whether it was her imagination she got a pedometer and learned it wasn't all in her head; she clocks in regularly at about fifteen miles a day—or was it five? In any case, it's a lot of walking without getting any place.

Mebbe I'd better not get a pedometer after all. If I find out for sure what my mileage is it may just depress me further, and I am already low in spirit after reading a survey on the worth of a woman who stays home and does housework, compared with one who has an outside job. According to the chart, at my age level, prorated on the number of hours I work, I am worth 66 cents an hour.

Biscuits and Birthday Cakes

Love my wife, love my baby,
Love my biscuits sopped in gravy.
   —"Black-Eyed Susie"

MY high hopes for the future of the nation took a slight dip recently. While looking over a late edition of the *Boy Scout Manual* I came across instructions for making campfire biscuits: "Just follow the directions on the box."

Shades of something or other! It's bad enough when a whole generation of cooks is conditioned to think that homemade means to open a package and put the contents in an oven. But things have really gotten out of hand when the motto "Be Prepared" translates into "Bring along a box of biscuit mix." Mercy, what would our pioneers, prospectors, and a long procession of good cooks make of this?

This nation was built on a solid foundation of biscuits: baking powder, soda, buttermilk, sourdough, beaten, risen, and the rest. The only "box" biscuits were those feather-light types that are somewhere in between a regular biscuit and a light roll. Our native biscuits evolved from the Scottish scone (pronounced to rhyme with John, not Joan). What the English call biscuits are, in fact, cookies, and if you think that's peculiar you should see what they call crackers! Not something to eat with soup or cheese but those party favors you pop open to pull out a funny hat.

But to get back to our biscuits. What else takes so little time to put together and can be made in so many different ways, or combined with so many other dishes? Come to think of it, what is better than just biscuits—split while they're hot, oozing with butter?

I've been baking biscuits since I was knee high to a grasshopper, or at least so little I had to stand on a box by the kitchen table to reach the dough board. Over the years I've baked them about every hour around the clock one time or another, and rolled them out on everything from the hood of an automobile to the top of the washing machine when no other flat space was available. In a pinch a piece of wax paper or foil can make do for a dough board. A round bottle makes an adequate rolling pin, and an empty tin or glass can be used as a cutter. The basic dough requires nothing more than flour, salt, a dab of shortening, liquid, and something to make it rise.

The best of all biscuits are made with buttermilk, but would you believe that many highly respected cookbooks don't even include a recipe for them? And of those that do, some call for the addition of sugar? (That really ties the rag on the bush, *sugar* in buttermilk biscuits!) For those who didn't grow up knowing how, or who use one of these misguided cookbooks, here's how to make real BUTTERMILK BISCUITS. Sift together 2 C flour, 1 tsp salt, and ½ tsp soda. With the fingers work in 2 to 4 T shortening, add enough buttermilk to make a soft dough, turn out on a floured board, knead for a minute or so, roll out ½ inch thick, cut into rounds, place on greased baking sheet, and bake for 15 minutes at 425°. The shortening can be butter, lard, or vegetable shortening; each will give a slightly different result. Try all three and see which you like best but *do* don't, in the words of Br'er Rabbit, go putting in sugar.

Since every cookbook of any scope includes a recipe for BAKING POWDER BISCUITS, it may be redundant to include a recipe, but here goes. Sift together 2 C flour, 1 tsp salt, and 2 tsp baking powder (*or* ¾ tsp soda and 1½ tsp cream of tartar). With fingers, rub in 2 T shortening and add enough sweet milk to make a soft dough. Turn out on floured board, roll, cut, and bake—just like buttermilk biscuits.

Although neither of these recipes takes more than about twenty minutes from start to table, biscuits do freeze well, and sometimes it is convenient to have them ready to heat and eat. Joan Holden, who lives up near Lincoln, has her good cook, Bessie, make up biscuits in huge batches to put in the freezer and take out to use any time someone gets hungry for them. When her daughter Kathy comes up from Richmond, she always takes back enough to last between visits. The other day she called to say they would have to come up right away; little Tacey hadn't found any Bessie Biscuits in the freezer and raised the roof.

Since I have thick country cream, I sometimes make CREAM BISCUITS. Sift together 2 C flour, 1 tsp salt, and 2 tsp baking powder. Mix in enough thick sweet cream to make a soft dough, knead, roll out, cut, and bake as usual. A version made with commercial sour cream is just as good; in this case substitute ½ tsp soda for the baking powder.

Once you've found a basic biscuit recipe that turns out well for you, there are all sorts of variations you can try. To make delicious PINWHEELS, roll dough about ½ inch thick, spread with some filling, roll up, slice, and bake. Fillings can be anything from minced ham, cooked and crumbled sausage, or grated cheese to sweet versions with marmalade, fruit butters, or cinnamon sugar.

Or the dough can be cut into strips and rolled around partially cooked link sausages or frankfurters that have been split and filled with some mustard, cheese, and Worcestershire sauce. These should be baked until light brown in a 375° oven.

Grated cheese can be added to the dry ingredients when mixing dough, or, for something even better and less usual, top each biscuit with a cube of sharp cheese before baking. You can fancy them up in a lot of other ways, but me, I'll take mine plain or sopped in gravy—either Red-Eye Gravy (page 188) to go with a slice of fried country ham or milk gravy that's been stirred up after the chicken is fried.

Recently I had a request for a very special birthday cake. To my way of thinking, all birthday cakes should be special. Some have been smashing, one was such a flop that our daughter Mace called it her pie-cake because it was "square like a cake, flat like a pie," but here are three cakes that are special enough for any birthday. In fact, they are so pretty and so good they can make a celebration out of any old day.

WILD ROSE CAKE is the one I recommended for Miss Mo, since her doting grandmother wanted to bake it in heart-shape pans. This amount makes 2 standard-size layers in any shape. Doubled, it would do for a large tube pan. One year I increased it enough to make a sheet cake that was almost 2 feet square and decorated the top with a flower garden of pastel candy mints. Some cake. But to get back to the beginning:

In large bowl of mixer beat 10 egg whites with a pinch of salt until stiff. Shift to another container, return bowl to mixer, and in it combine 1 C butter with 3 C granulated sugar and beat at high speed until light and fluffy. Turn speed down and add alternately 1 C milk mixed with 1 T rose water and 4 C sifted cake flour which has been resifted with 3 tsp baking powder. When batter is smooth, mix in enough red food coloring to tint it a soft rosy pink. Finally, fold in the beaten egg whites, turn into two prepared layer pans, and bake at 350° for about 25 minutes. When cake is done, cool on racks; then fill and ice with seven-minute frosting which has been flavored with almond extract. This cake can be decorated with two or three real Sweetheart roses, or with sugar roses that have been tinted a delicate pink. Remember, go easy on the color, for both cake and decoration.

DAISY CAKE starts with white layers. In bowl of mixer beat 6 egg whites with a pinch of salt until stiff. Switch to another container, return bowl to mixer, combine 1 C butter with 2 C sugar, and beat at high speed until fluffy and light. Add 1 tsp vanilla to ¾ C milk and add alternately with 3 C sifted flour, resifted with ½ tsp soda and 1 tsp cream of tartar, mixing at medium speed. When batter is smooth, fold in egg whites, pour into 2 lightly greased and floured layer pans (about 7-inch size), and bake at 350° for about 25 minutes.

While cake is baking make filling. In heat-proof bowl or top of double boiler combine 6 egg yolks with 1 C sugar and the juice and grated rind of 1 lemon. Cook and stir over boiling water until it is thick enough to spread. Spread cooled filling on cool cake layers and ice with seven-minute frosting flavored with vanilla. Decorate with "Daisy" candy mints.

For ORANGE FROST CAKE an electric mixer is essential. In large mixer bowl combine 4 whole eggs with 2 C granulated sugar and beat at high speed for at least 12 minutes. While this is mixing combine 1 C milk with ½ tsp almond flavoring, bring to boil, and remove from heat. Sift together 2 C sifted cake flour with 2 tsp baking powder. When sugar-egg mixture is ready, turn mixer speed down and slowly add flour mixture. When this batter is smooth, slowly add warm flavored milk and beat for 3 minutes. Turn into 2 prepared layer pans and bake about 25 minutes at 350°.

When cake layers are baked and cool, cover top of each with seven-minute icing that has been flavored with vanilla. (Put aside, covered, in a warm place, enough icing to coat sides of cake later.) *Do not put layers of cake together at this stage.* While the icing on the cake layers is firming up, mix the orange-frost topping. Combine 2 T sugar and 2 C coconut flakes with the juice, pulp, and grated rind of a large orange. Toss lightly with a fork to mix thoroughly. When icing begins to set, put ½ the orange-frost mixture on top of each layer of cake. Put layers together, spread reserved icing around sides, and make a thick rim of icing around top edge. If candles are used, space them around the iced rim. The methods of mixing and combining ingredients of this cake are both unusual, the result is delicious.

Foretaste of Spring

I wonder if the sap is stirring yet,
If wintry birds are dreaming of a mate,
If frozen snowdrops feel as yet the sun,
And crocus fires are kindling one by one.
—Christina Rossetti

WE missed out on the January thaw but February has made up for it. Several days of balmy weather—and at least one with an all-time record-breaking temperature of 76°—brought a lot of incautious green shoots pushing through the ground, started the sap to rising and the buds to swelling.

In years past this would have been the time to cut branches of miniature pussy willow that grew along the little stream in front. Since it was growing here on the place I assumed it was common and never bothered to root cuttings for additional plants of it. Now, it has disappeared—possibly crowded out by larger plants or a change in the streambed—and I can't find more anywhere. Too bad, for it was charming, especially in arrangements with miniature daffodils and other small-flowering bulbs. The stems naturally grew in interesting curves, and the tiny gray "pussies" weren't much larger than a grain of wheat.

Closer to the house the black-catkin willow (*Salix melanostachys*) is beginning to open, and what an interesting small tree it is. The stems are a glowing red and the plump little pussies have coal-black "fur." This is a very choice and rare plant, and when I was lucky enough to get a rooted cutting of it I gave it tender loving care and, as soon as it was large enough, propagated several other plants from it, just to be on the safe side.

Down by the edge of the pond the fantail willow should be ready to force so I'll cut a few today. The deer that come to the pond always stop to browse on this small tree, but fortunately they can't reach the branches that extend out over the water. For this reason the tree doesn't have as nice a form as it should—in fact, it is downright lopsided—but at least I get a few branches to use in arrangements.

The furry buds on the star magnolia are much larger than these others and have a soft grayish green color that looks perfect in the gray stone container Peter Connors of Middleburg chiseled out of a chunk of rock.

Out along the edge of the woods the hazelnut catkins are also ready to cut. All these things can be cut now and dried for use throughout the season.

As for the snowdrops, they are not only feeling the sun, most of them are in full bloom. These are such satisfactory little bulbs. Nothing seems to bother them, and if they are planted in protected spots—nestled at the base of trees, or under sheltering branches of shrubs and evergreens—they will soon start reseeding themselves and go roaming all over the place. There is something so fresh and pretty about the green and white flowers, one couldn't have too many of them. I have several different species, all nice, but the tiny double ones are especially appealing.

One of the loveliest things on the place right now is the silver maple filled with clusters of rusty-red buds. When a chickadee lights on a limb, the shades of gray, black, and white against the gray bark and velvety red buds make a picture that might be found in a Japanese print, but here it is, right outside the kitchen window.

The silver maple is definitely a "weed" tree. Fast growing, it *does* provide some shade much sooner than slow-growing trees, but the shallow roots make it impossible to grow anything under and around it. Then the seed capsules come showering down by the bushel and take root wherever they land. If gutters aren't cleaned out soon after the seeds fall, the next thing you know you have a hedge of maples growing along the roof line. Later, when the leaves fall, they just lie there in a sodden mass, smothering grass and cultivated plants if they aren't swept up and carted to the compost—most annoying to those of us

50 / *February*

who aren't fanatic leaf-sweepers. But right now, all is forgiven for they are so beautiful.

We had roast turkey on Sunday and I wanted to use some of the leftovers for a DUTCH COUNTRY CASSEROLE, a recipe I worked out after eating the famous Pennsylvania Dutch chicken soup they serve up around York and Lancaster. (*Now* they have a version of it printed on the noodle package but I go on making it my way, which I think is better.) In 3 quarts of boiling, salted water cook one 12-ounce package of the large square noodles about 30 minutes, stirring occasionally to keep them from sticking. When the noodles are tender, drain, rinse with hot water, and drain again. Put half of them in the bottom of a shallow baking pan that has been well buttered. Cover with a layer of cooked chicken or turkey cut into largish chunks, add 2 C frozen corn, ½ C each chopped onion and celery, 1 green pepper cut into thin strips, and about ½ C minced fresh parsley. Add top layer of noodles and pour over this 2 C chicken or turkey broth that has been seasoned with salt, freshly ground pepper, and celery salt—and just a dash of Tabasco to give it a little zip. Sprinkle with buttered crumbs and about ½ C wheat germ. Bake at 350° about 40 minutes.

In addition to the Dutch Country Casserole, this turkey provided slices for serving cold with some of my glorified Mango-Peach Chutney (page 135) and some sandwiches. There was enough for a soup—at the end—some hash just before the last act, and Turkey Sub Gum before then.

To make TURKEY SUB GUM combine 4 ribs celery, cut in thin slices on the slant, with 1 medium onion chopped in medium-size pieces, and add to 2 C chicken or turkey broth in a large skillet. Cover, bring to boil, and simmer for 5 minutes. Add 1 large green pepper that has been seeded, cut in quarters, and sliced across in ¼-inch strips. Cover and simmer 5 minutes more. Add 4 T soy sauce and 3 C cooked chicken or turkey cut into ½-inch cubes, and cover but turn off heat. Just before serving add 1

Foretaste of Spring /51

can water chestnuts cut into thin slices and ½ C slivered almonds. Heat until simmering, add 2 tsp cornstarch dissolved in a small amount of water or broth, and continue to cook, stirring gently, until sauce is thick and clear. Serve with rice and crisp chow mein noodles. It is definitely nontraditional, but with this I frequently serve chilled Watermelon Pickle (page 135) and get no complaints.

PLUM SAUCE is more usually served with oriental-type dishes, but it is also good with a number of other things, including cold roast meats and fowl. Combine ½ C finely chopped chutney with 1 C red plum jam and 1 T each brown sugar and vinegar. Heat gently to blend flavors; then cover and store in refrigerator.

On the twenty-fifth of February the first daffodils were in bloom, all my own miniature seedlings whose ancestors are among the earliest species to appear, frequently found flowering in ice and snow on high mountains in Spain, Portugal, and France. These were planted in a protected spot on the south side of the greenhouse, but elsewhere, in other locations, other bulbs are well up and showing color. I hope no one gets lulled into a sense of false security by this unprecedented weather. Ten years ago, about this time, we had our worst snowstorm and blizzard on record, with drifts thirty feet high in some places. And a mild and balmy April Fool's Day last year was followed on the weekend by frigid windstorms and sleet.

What to do about these early flowers that are coming along before their appointed time? Well, not very much. If beds have been well mulched, this will prevent the alternate freezing and thawing which causes heaving and consequent damage to plants. If you have just a few things to protect, a light covering of something that won't pack down, like oak leaves or even evergreen branches, will help —or at least it won't hurt. But if you have any large plantings in a number of locations, about the only thing you can do is to cross everything, including your eyes, and hope for the best.

I must say I *do* have protective feelings about these

miniature daffodils, they look so tiny and defenseless. The little yellow ones, now in bloom, aren't more than two inches tall, and the flowers are about the size of the end of my little finger. One, just a bit taller with a larger flower, is pure white, with perfect form. This one definitely goes on the list of those to be registered and introduced.

In checking over the early planted seed in the greenhouse, I have to conclude that my Pixie is pixilated. On January 17 I planted seed of Pixie Tomato. Cherry and Golden Ponderosa planted two weeks later are now up and of a size to transplant, while only a couple of Pixies have germinated and they are just standing there sulking.

MARCH
Deceptive March Days

March comes in like a lion and goes out like a lamb.
—Old saying

BUT what about when March comes in like a lamb? Well, there's another old saying that goes, "Start off mild—end up wild." We can't fool ourselves into thinking this is the real thing. In our hearts we know there can be a lot of bluster and blow—or even a blizzard or two—before spring really arrives and decides to stay.

Meanwhile, in several places the old, early trumpet daffodils have dared to come and brave the winds of March. These are probably the same ones Shakespeare wrote about. In England they're called Lent lilies, in some places they're called Easter flowers, and around here we know them as Early Virginia. They were brought over by some of the first settlers, but a lot of people think of them as being native wildflowers, for they are found growing in the woods and along roadsides as well as in old gardens and farm dooryards.

Out under the buckeye tree the snowdrops are about finished, but the air is sweet with the little fragrant iris. In the catalogs these are listed as *Iris reticulata.* There are some so-called improved varieties, but these purple species have the sweetest scent, cost the least, and are generally the most satisfactory for the garden.

Everywhere crocus is in bloom: white, gold, and shades of lavender, mauve, and purple—that is, they're in bloom everywhere the chipmunks haven't eaten the bulbs. Out in the vegetable garden there is enough upland cress —creasy greens—to make a meal, and a lot of trees and shrubs are bustin' out. There are even a few flowers on the star magnolia, and all the willows have turned a misty green.

There are also some new arrivals on the bird scene. A boat-tailed grackle has come back for the third year in a row. One expert birder insists that this bird just does not appear around here, but this one does and it is so distinctive it can't be confused with the common grackles that hang around all winter.

A great flock of sparrows that flew in and spent a few hours scratching around in the leaves, softly chirping, *did* have me puzzled. If anyone thinks a sparrow is a sparrow and an English one at that, think again. There are more than fifty species, and a lot of them are more confusing than the Confusing Fall Warblers. All winter we have had song sparrows, white-crowns, whitethroats, occasional fox sparrows, and some others, but these were different. I finally gave up, stopped trying to identify them, and just enjoyed watching and listening to them.

I *did* identify the killdee up at the shopping center, east of Leesburg. This crazy mixed-up bird must have once laid her eggs in the open field that *was* and persists in trying to continue the practice on the parking lot that *is*. The killdee doesn't build a regular nest but, with a sort of touching faith, drops her eggs in open pastures, on plowed ground, or even between rows in the garden. Numerous times I have watched this particular one wandering around the paved lot like someone who has lost something and is looking for it. I wish she'd have enough sense to move along to some more suitable place to lay her eggs. She worries me, and I already have enough things to worry about.

Last week I left the place long enough to go on safari down to Reston to give a garden club program. Asked for a native guide to meet me at Route 7 and lead the way to the meeting place, and a good thing I did for I would never have found it on my own. As it was I couldn't even find my way back out again. Going back and forth between Reston and Herndon I began to feel as though I had been consigned to the Houseboat on the Styx, going to and coming from, but never landing. Eventually I got back home but still don't know how I did it.

Am ashamed to admit it but I can't even seem to get around the bypass and on west without recircling back through Leesburg three or four times. Road signs were not designed for the likes of me, and when there is any deviation from an accustomed route I just can't get there from here. When someone gives directions and says "You can't miss it," that's a sure sign I'm not going to find it.

These warm days must have turned my thoughts to summertime meals. The other night we had a dinner that

Deceptive March Days

might have come from the garden, except for a few strips of crisp bacon: fried tomatoes, whole new potatoes boiled and dressed with fresh parsley and butter, and frozen corn that tasted almost like fresh, cooked with a green pepper and a bit of bacon drippings.

Another night I stretched the budget and splurged on the first fresh asparagus to reach the market. With it we had an omelet and bread, hot from the oven. Was feeling a bit guilty about spending so much on one vegetable for one meal; then realized that, all considered, this meal wasn't as expensive as a couple of TV dinners would have been.

Perhaps it's a matter of conditioning and having started to cook and market during the Depression, but I simply can't bring myself to pay the prices that some things cost now. As for the TV dinners—to date we've never had one. A few times I've been so tired I've been tempted, but then I remember the egg and opt for an omelet—just as easy, so much better, and it takes much less time. A plain omelet is pretty good fare any time. When you fold it around some filling and add some sauce and cheese, you've got the main dish for a meal.

Tossing around an omelet seems to be a favorite indoor sport on television programs. A lot of stirring and pan twirling does make an interesting act to watch, but I follow a different procedure. Since it was taught me by a fine French cook, I guess it could be called a FRENCH OMELET. To begin with I have a well-seasoned 7-inch omelet pan, not expensive and not fancy looking, just plain aluminum with sloping sides. Nothing except an omelet is ever cooked in it, and it is never washed—just wiped out with a paper towel after use. If an omelet pan *has* to be washed or scoured, then it has to be seasoned again.

No matter how many servings are necessary, a single two-egg omelet is made for each. In a small bowl, using a silver fork, beat 2 eggs with 2 T cream, some coarse salt, freshly ground pepper, a dash of Tabasco, and probably some minced herbs. Stir a lump of butter around the hot omelet pan until it is well coated. Add egg mixture. As it cooks, push edges to center of pan, letting liquid run to sides. When top is still quite soft and fairly runny, spoon on filling, fold two sides over middle, and turn out on a hot serving plate. Spoon on sauce and sprinkle with cheese.

One OMELET SAUCE I make a lot is used for filling *and* topping the omelet. In a small amount of oil or butter simmer 1 chopped onion until limp and then add some chopped green pepper and celery, 2 C chopped fresh or canned tomatoes, 1 tsp molasses, salt and pepper to taste, and a sprig of sweet basil. Cook, uncovered, about 10 minutes. Add 1 C fresh or frozen peas or chopped zucchini, cover, and simmer 5 minutes longer. Thicken, if necessary, with a little cornstarch dissolved in cold water.

Since I was a minority of one for my birthday dinner, I didn't bother to bake a cake and sing "Happy Birthday" to myself. Dispensing with the song I will bake the cake this weekend, since Old Sweet Tooth Himself got carried away and gave me *two* portable radios with a decent tone —one for the kitchen, another for my bedside. Thank you, thank you.

Since we haven't had one for some time I guess I'll go for a rich DEVIL'S FOOD CAKE. In small mixer bowl cream ½ C butter with 1 C brown sugar until light and fluffy. Set aside and in larger bowl combine 2 eggs with 1 C brown sugar and mix at high speed for 5 minutes. Add creamed mixture and mix until well blended. Turn mixer to low speed; add alternately 2 C sifted cake flour and 1 tsp each baking powder and salt, resifted together, ¾ C buttermilk, and ¼ C strong coffee essence. At last fold in 4 squares melted bitter chocolate and 1 tsp rum. Turn into 2 greased and floured layer pans or a single sheet pan. Bake at 325°: 30 minutes for layers, a bit longer for a single sheet. With this I think a rich chocolate icing is too much of a good thing and prefer a thin butter icing flavored with rum or fresh lemon rind and juice.

As usual I received one birthday card and as usual it came from my friendly chiropractor, reminding me that

I am a year older and my back isn't getting any younger. He started the custom years ago, after the summer I threw my back out trying to heave manure with a silo fork. For anyone unfamiliar with a silo fork, it is just as long but about four times as wide as a standard pitchfork. I got the bright idea of using one when I was trying to spread a pile of manure over the garden and wasn't making much headway with the pitchfork.

At the first forkful that I tried to lift something snapped and there I was immobilized, bent over like a hairpin, too far from the house for anyone to hear my cries for help. I might have died out there and had to be buried in a round coffin, but finally I got to the house.

When everything else failed to straighten me out I went to the chiropractor. This happened years ago and I haven't been back since; when my back starts to give me trouble I just remember all those snaps, crackles, and pops along my spine and feel better immediately. But it's nice to know he still *cares*.

A Mess of Pottage and a Cottage Loaf

Jacob gave Esau bread and pottage of lentiles; and he did eat and drink.
—Genesis 25:34

WHETHER your mess of pottage is "a strong broth of meat with herbs and spices boyled" or a thick soup of lentils, split peas, or beans, it will make a meal that sticks to the ribs and gives you a warm glow of well-being. Pottage was the original one-dish meal, and nothing since then has pushed it out of favor. Some version of it is central to the cuisine of almost every country. When we lived down in Southwest Virginia it was indeed a poor sort of kitchen that didn't have a pot of bean soup simmering on the back of a woodburning stove, and they say the most popular item on the menu at the Senate Dining Room is that same celebrated bean soup.

Whether you're cooking for one or for a crowd, a pot of hearty soup is easy and inexpensive to make, and you can be doing all sorts of other interesting or essential things while it is cooking. It can be kept on "hold" if mealtime has to be a movable feast, or stretched to provide extra servings if necessary, and leftovers—if any—are even better when reheated for another meal.

In making MIXED VEGETABLE SOUP I never follow a set recipe but just toss in whatever comes to mind that I have on hand or can scrounge from the garden. Each version comes out different; all are good. (You can't go far wrong with almost any combination of vegetables.) I might start with a meaty soupbone (remember when your friendly butcher just threw these in with your order, for free?), add a quart jar of my tomatoes with herbs, and go on from there.

The other day the soup base was 1 C dried white beans, put on to simmer early in about 1 pint of water. (If you have hard water you have to allow extra time for dried beans to cook.) After about an hour I added 2 C tomatoes (the other half of a jar that had been opened the day before) and a succession of peeled and sliced or diced vegetables on hand: onion, carrot, turnip, potato, and a couple of ribs of celery. Then, from the garden, a large Winter Keeper beet, a knob of celery root, peeled and chopped leaf ribs of the purple cauliflower that never got around to "flowering," and a Jerusalem artichoke. At this stage the plot was thickening so I added water, along with about ¼ C dried corn and 2 C ham broth from the freezer.

When this had all simmered along for a while I started seasoning: coarse salt, freshly ground pepper, a small hot pepper, celery salt, about 1 T molasses, some stems of fresh parsley, a bay leaf, and some celery leaves. (Other herbs, especially thyme and marjoram, are also good additions.) Then I beefed it up by adding 1 C chopped, leftover ham. Close to serving time it seemed a bit thin, so I threw in a handful of thin spaghetti broken into short lengths.

With leftover beef or lamb I would have used a beef extract, or a chicken concentrate with turkey trimmings. Noodles, rice, or barley might have replaced the pasta—but the two latter would have required longer cooking time.

Frequently my choice of pottage depends on how much time there is to get a meal together. LENTIL SOUP is ready in less than an hour; SPLIT PEA SOUP takes very little longer. To 1 pound of either I add 1 chopped onion and 1 carrot, 4 C water and 2 C ham broth, 1 C chopped ham, 1 small red pepper, celery leaves, fresh parsley, and salt, pepper, and celery salt to taste toward the end of the cooking time. If the finished soup is too thick, I thin it down or extend it by adding water, broth, or rich milk. (I do not put it through a food mill or sieve as some recipes recommend.)

Likewise, elapsed time determines the type of bread I serve with these hearty soups. Either cornmeal or bran muffins are good and take only about 30 minutes to put together and bake. Hush Puppies (page 19) require even less time. Until quite recently I was a Hush Puppy Snob and looked down my nose on any recipe that called for anything other than water-ground cornmeal, salt, and boiling water. Well, the other day I got carried away and tossed some dried onion flakes and chopped green tops of fresh onion in with the meal and salt, before adding the water. The darned things were *good*. So I'll have to eat my words, and eat crow, and admit these onion-adders had a good idea all along.

If I have a couple of hours or so to make it, my first choice for bread to go with pottage is a Cottage Loaf, sliced and eaten while warm, with plenty of fresh sweet butter. To make COTTAGE LOAF, heat 1½ C water until very warm to touch. Pour ½ C of the warm water in small bowl or large cup, add 2 T granulated dry yeast (which I buy in quantity at a health food store) and 1 tsp brown sugar, and stir to mix. While this is working, pour the rest of the water in a large mixing bowl, add 2 tsp coarse salt, and stir in 1 C whole wheat flour. Add the yeast mixture as soon as it is foamy, stir, and mix in 3 C unbleached white flour. Turn dough out on floured board or marble slab and knead until smooth, adding flour as necessary to keep dough from sticking. When smooth, lightly flour ball of dough and turn into a crock or mixing bowl that has been filled with boiling water, drained, and wiped completely dry. *Do not grease bowl.*

Cover bowl with damp tea towel, cover towel with plastic to hold in moisture and heat, and set aside in a warm place. When the dough has doubled in bulk, about 1 hour, turn out on floured board, punch down, form into smooth ball, and place in a clean, dry, flowerpot saucer (7 or 8 inches across the top) that has been lightly greased and dusted with coarse cornmeal. Let rise, covered, in warm place and bake about 40 minutes at 400°.

You can vary the texture by adding ¼ C wheat germ or bulgur (cracked wheat) along with the whole wheat flour, but this makes a marvelous chewy loaf with a thick, crunchy crust just as is.

To make my unsenatorial version of SENATE BEAN SOUP, sort and wash 1 pound great northern beans. Add about 6 C water, cover, bring to boil, and simmer. Check from time to time and add water as necessary. After about 1 hour add 2 C ham broth, 1 onion stuck with 1 clove, and some celery leaves. Continue to add water as necessary, and after simmering for another hour add 1 small hot pepper, coarse salt, freshly ground pepper, a sprig of fresh sweet basil and some fresh parsley, and 1 C or so of chopped ham.

Meanwhile, in a separate pan cook 1 large mealy potato that has been peeled, quartered, and covered with water. When potato is soft, coarsely mash with a fork, right in the potato water, and set aside, covered. When beans are done, fish out trailing stems of herbs, add mashed potato and water, use additional broth or water if the soup is too thick, and adjust seasoning to taste.

For an unauthentic but very good FYSHE POTTAGE, i.e., clam or fish chowder, dice 3 slices lean bacon or a ¼-inch slice of salt pork and cook slowly in a large saucepan. When crisp, remove meat with slotted spoon and set aside to drain on paper towel. Put 1 chopped onion in fat remaining in pan, cover, and cook slowly until onion is wilted. Add about 3 C peeled, diced potatoes, pour in clam juice, fish stock, or chicken broth just to cover, and cook slowly, covered, until potatoes are done. Add 3 cans minced clams or 1 pound cod or haddock fillet that has been poached and separated into large flakes, coarse salt, freshly ground pepper, and enough light cream to make a thick soup. Heat; then just before serving add the crisp bacon or pork bits and sprinkle with paprika.

A really good stock or stew pot is not inexpensive, but it can be about your best investment in kitchen equipment when you consider all the things you can do with it in addition to making soups and stews. Mine is stainless steel for easy care and no off-odors or colors when cooking certain foods, with a heavy aluminum base that gives efficient, steady heat and fits *flat* on the element of an electric stove, which makes for a great saving in fuel. Since I am usually at home and can watch the pot I don't have one of these new electric crock cookers, but they are ideal for anyone who leaves the kitchen after breakfast and doesn't get back until dinnertime, and they should turn out wonderful soups.

Beans, Beans, Beans

I never met a bean I didn't like.

—Jim Birchfield

IF you are what you eat, then I am a Bean and come from a long line of Beans. Further, I married a Bean who came from a long line of Beans. This does not make us all that unusual, considering the universal appeal and conspicuous consumption of different types of beans, but we may be a bit more than normally dedicated to the proposition that the Bean is Supreme. Red or yellow, black or white—not to mention green, brown, pink, purple, or blue; speckled, plain, or striped—all are handsome in our sight and a fair treat to eat.

Even the names roll off like a litany to good eating. French flageolets, Mexican frijoles, English broad or fava beans, Swedish brown beans, California pink beans; butter beans, limas, and baby limas; October, Jacob's cattle, navy, pea, great northern beans; bird's egg, pinto, or kidney beans; snap, string, shell, and rattail beans; Haricot, Blue Lake, Kentucky Wonder; Yellow Wax, Lazy Wife, Old Homestead; Creaseback, Blue Coco; Cornhill, King of the Garden, Fordhook, Red Valentine; marrowfat, soy, mung; et cetera, et cetera, et cetera.

Boiled, baked, fried and refried, pickled, stewed, steamed, or roasted—from soup to nuts, including salad, side dishes, and main event—one could have an entire meal consisting of nothing but beans, just beans. Then there are all the "beans and" dishes: Hopping John, succotash, beans and corn, pork and beans, beans and beef, chili with beans, beans with cheese, and cassoulet (a rich, succulent combination of beans, mutton, goose, and several sausages).

In New England, Boston Baked Beans and Brown Bread are as inevitable as Saturday night. What a good idea it is to have one meal a week that doesn't vary. If it happens to be B.B.B. & B.B. night, the cook is kitchen-liberated all day and the evening meal can be a movable feast, a sort of serve-yourself-when-you're-ready-to-eat affair (a great boon in families where everyone seems to be operating on a different schedule, involved in different activities). It doesn't wreck the food budget if you prepare enough extra to feed potluck guests, and if you have any leftovers you have the makings for one or two additional meals or Baked Bean Sandwiches for Sunday supper.

For my UN-BOSTON BAKED BEANS, pick over and wash 1 pound of great northern beans. Combine with 2 quarts of water in a large pan, cover, and cook at low heat for 1 hour. Meanwhile, prepare meat—1 pound or so of fresh lean pork, cut into 2-inch chunks—and in a separate bowl mix together 2 T each coarse salt, prepared mustard, and brown sugar; ⅓ C molasses; and 4 T homemade Chili Sauce (page 139). At end of parboiling time, ladle half the beans into a regular 2-quart baking dish that has a tight-fitting cover. Cover with the pork chunks and stick in 2 or 3 whole peeled onions. Add the rest of the beans. Mix the prepared seasonings with bean water and pour over the beans. Cover and bake at about 250° for 5 hours, adding more water if necessary during cooking time. At the end of 5 hours remove cover and continue to bake for another hour.

For BAKED BEAN SANDWICHES, just slightly mash the cold baked beans, heap onto slices of homemade whole wheat bread, add a spoonful of homemade Chili Sauce, and serve Bread and Butter Pickles (page 138) on the side.

As for the BROWN BREAD to go with them, mixing up a batch takes a matter of minutes and requires absolutely no skill. In a bowl, dump 1 C each of water-ground cornmeal, rye or white flour, and whole wheat flour. Add ¾ T soda, 1 tsp salt, ¾ C molasses, 2 C buttermilk, and 1 C raisins. Stir until thoroughly mixed, fill greased tins (any size) no more than ⅔ full, cover with aluminum foil, and steam: quart tins for 3 hours, pint tins 2 hours, smaller sizes 1 hour. Serve hot, sliced, with or without butter. Any bread left over can be served cold, sliced thin, and spread with softened cream cheese—good with soups or salads.

Just as traditional, but not nearly as well known, is the bean dish called LEATHER BRITCHES. In fact, what with modern methods and facilities for freezing and canning, making Leather Britches is almost a lost art. A pity, for they are *some* good eating. You start with fresh green beans (Kentucky Wonder or some other flat bean is best). Wash, string, and break the beans into good-size lengths; then with a darning needle thread them onto cotton twine (just like stringing beads) and hang to dry in a warm place—above a coal or wood range was the favored spot for drying. When the Leather Britches are completely dry, store them in airtight containers. Before cooking, soak them overnight in water to cover, then cook gently until tender and use a small chunk of fatback to season them.

If it takes shortages to bring us back to food like this, then perhaps the shortages are a good thing. You *know* what is in the food because you put it there; it contains no hidden horrors; it is simple, sustaining, and inexpensive; the flavor is beyond anything you can buy in a "convenience" cooking bag; and it brings back an ingredient that is missing in too many modern kitchens—the marvelous aroma and fragrance of good food in the making.

Sparragrass and a Good Cheese Companion

> *Take young Sparragrass, tye it up in bunches: when your Skillet boyle, put in enough to make a dish; when it is boyled and drained, dish it up; pour on butter and vinegar and send it up.*
> —*Seventeenth-century cookery book*

UNTIL taking root here on "the forty acres" I had never planted asparagus. It can't be cut until two or three years after planting, and by that time we would probably have moved on. There just didn't seem to be much point in putting in an asparagus bed for the future pleasure of someone else. But when we bought land and appeared to be settled down in one place, I put in an asparagus bed that made up for lost time: eight 50-foot rows, planted in trenches 3 feet deep, with some drainage material and about 2 feet of manure, topped off with rich soil in which to set the roots.

When the crops started coming in a couple of years later, it became obvious that I had bitten off more asparagus than the five of us could chew. After struggling to keep up with it for about six weeks of every season, several seasons, I stopped cultivating and fertilizing it and let nature take over. Eventually it produced only a few stray spears from time to time.

Now we have two small beds, 15 feet by 30 inches, in which Waltham asparagus roots were planted just the way one would plant any perennial, set a foot apart each way. It is easy to keep these beds weeded, well-manured, mulched, and fertilized. They produce a reasonable supply for eating fresh during the season. If we have a hankering for it out of season, when it is expensive, I succumb to temptation and don't even look at the price. After all, we can do without a lot of necessities, but we must have some of the luxuries.

In cooking asparagus I don't "tye it up in bunches," but I do in the "Skillet boyle"—in a special way. After selecting thick spears of the same size I break off tough ends, remove scales, and rinse in cold water before storing them in the refrigerator in a plastic bag to keep crisp. A few of the tough ends are washed and reserved and, at cooking time, arranged along one side of a large, heavy skillet, to keep the tips of the first row of spears from being in water. Additional rows are arranged in layers, with the tips supported by the preceding layer. After adding about ½ C water the skillet is covered and brought to a boil and then the heat is turned off. In a few minutes I test a spear with the tip of a paring knife. It should be just tender but not the least bit limp.

Asparagus is correctly eaten as a finger food. To quote from the etiquette section of an old cookbook, "Asparagus should be taken from the finger and thumb; if it is fit to set before you, the whole of it may be eaten." When I am served spears of asparagus that are too limp to be lifted with the fingers I assume the hostess probably doesn't know how it should be eaten and certainly doesn't know how it should be cooked.

Simply dressed with melted butter, coarse salt, and freshly ground pepper is good enough for me, but now that I have a Tricer I can get fancy occasionally and serve ASPARAGUS WITH HOLLANDAISE SAUCE. Using a plastic or steel knife, put 3 egg yolks, 2 tsp lemon juice, ½ tsp coarse salt, and a dash of Tabasco in bowl, cover, but remove pusher from feed tube. In a small saucepan heat ½ C sweet butter until it begins to bubble. Turn on machine and immediately pour in hot butter. Turn off immediately, scrape sauce into a small bowl, and keep warm over hot water until serving time.

If asparagus spears are not thick or of the same size, prepare them in a different way. After breaking off the tough ends and removing the scales, cut spears into slanting ½-inch slices, reserving tips, add a small amount of water to slices, cover and cook until not quite tender, drop in the tips, and continue cooking for 1 minute or so.

However the asparagus is cooked, a good dish to go with it is a fake cheese soufflé, or what should probably be called a *strada*. By any name it is delicious and goes well with a number of other dishes: green beans vinaigrette, fried tomatoes, or just a mixed green salad. It must be assembled at least an hour before cooking time, but it *can* remain on "hold" in the refrigerator all day, or all night and half the day—a definite advantage during the busy days of spring and summer when we want to spend as much time as possible out in the garden. Mixing the ingredients takes a matter of minutes. It can be baked in a standard soufflé dish, but I prefer an oval gratin pan because it increases the amount of crusty top and sides. The size of the pan selected depends on the amount being made.

Here is the basic recipe for a STRADA that serves 3 or 4. (It can be halved or doubled with equally good results.)

Sparragrass and a Good Cheese Companion /67

In a well-buttered pan or baking dish put 4 slices of good bread that have been buttered and cut into 1-inch squares. Beat together 2 eggs, 2 C milk, and seasoning. (In addition to coarse salt, freshly ground pepper, and a dash of Tabasco I sometimes add herbs.) Pour this mixture over bread cubes and top it off with 2 C shredded sharp cheese. Press cheese down so liquid covers it. Let stand at least 1 hour and bake at 350° from 25 to around 40 minutes, depending on size. It should be puffed and crusty on top.

If you make Hollandaise Sauce, a good thing to do with those leftover egg whites is to make a MERINGUE TART, one of those desserts that look and taste elegant but are simple to put together. In the bowl of a mixer combine 3 egg whites with a pinch each of salt and cream of tartar. Beat until stiff; then continue to beat while slowly adding, alternately, 1 C sugar and a combination of 1 tsp each of water, vinegar, and flavoring. If you want to make a large tart, heap mixture on a lightly buttered baking sheet and with spatula form into a round "shell" with slightly raised sides. For individual tarts, shape portions into smaller shells, about 4 inches across. Bake large tart at 275° for about 1 hour, same temperature but less time for the smaller ones.

Just before serving fill shell with fresh sweetened fruit that has been flavored with liqueur and top with whipped cream. Or fill the shell with flavored whipped cream and add a circle of fresh fruit around the edge: raspberries, strawberries, sliced kiwi fruit, peaches, or whatever strikes your fancy. The smaller tarts can be filled with fruit, but they are also especially good filled with a serving of ice cream topped with a sweet sauce.

The Second Season

APRIL
Everything Happens in Spring

If a Footman take mugwort and put it into his shoes in the morning, he may goe forty miles before Noon and not be weary.
—The Art of Simpling, 1656

FROM the way my feet and crazy-legs felt last night, I had better put some mugwort in *my* shoes. What with the sun warming things up, the spring peepers peeping, the birds in a frenzy of nest building, all nature busting out all over —I get carried away, trying to do too many things out in the garden, and when it's time to come in and cook dinner I'm really the Draggin' Lady.

It was a good thing we had enough cold lamb left over to slice and serve; I just couldn't have started a meal from scratch. Lamb roasted with garlic is a classic combination, but for something special try lamb with fresh wild garlic. Slice the bulbs and insert them in the meat; then cut the tops into 3- or 4-inch lengths and lay them over the top of the roast after it has been seasoned. When the meat is done the garlic tops are crisp and crunchy. Mighty good!

To go with it, I found enough fresh young leaves of upland cress—creasy greens—to make a green salad. Before long there will be dandelion, mustard, and all the other good potherbs. One of the Rites of Spring is collecting these "greens"—but *be sure you know what you're getting.*

Several people have asked questions about fertilizer. If you use a balanced fertilizer get 5–10–10, which provides more potash than 5–10–5. The extra potash helps plants resist cold, heat, and disease, cuts down on water requirements, and speeds up growth. (Old-timers who dusted cut potatoes with wood ash before planting were on the right track. If you have no wood ashes, then use greensand or granite dust, good mineral sources of potash.) It's also a good idea to let cut potatoes air-dry 24 hours before dusting and planting; this allows them to form a sort of callus that protects from possible rot or disease. Do not lime soil where potatoes are to be planted (radishes and watermelons are two others that like acid soil), and do not plant potatoes where tomatoes were grown the previous year (they're in the same family and subject to many of the same diseases). Furrows for planting potatoes should be no more than 5 inches deep—then just sit back and wait until the first tiny new potatoes are ready to eat with the first batch of garden peas.

A liquid fertilizer is good for foliar feeding, fertilizing seedlings, and to give a good start to young plants being set out in the garden. I use fish emulsion and a liquid seaweed, which not only add important trace elements but act as soil conditioners as well.

Nest-building rites are going on all over the place. It even begins to look like we may have a resident goose, nesting on the island in the pond. In years past, Canada geese have come and gone, and this year, for the first time, a handsome pair appears to be staying. If I know anything about geese, these goosely visits to the island are for the purpose of laying eggs.

The egg-laying schedule for a goose is usually every other day. If you leave a "nest egg"—which can be something as implausible as an old light bulb—you can remove the fresh eggs as they are laid, to encourage higher production. Otherwise, as the eggs increase in the nest, the goose becomes "broody," stops laying, and starts setting.

Hatching time varies, according to breed. If nothing happens to break up the nest, Canada goslings usually pop out, twenty-eight days on the button, from the time the goose started setting. This will all be fun to watch—if don't nothin' happen.

The Carolina wren came back and was *furious.* You never heard such a fuss—not just when she discovered that her old nesting site had been "renovated" but all the time she spent building a new nest. Now she is settled down and quietly brooding. (Our lattice-covered frame around the bathroom window is a perfect protected spot for a small nest, but the old nest had to go when we took down the frame to be painted.)

All this nesting activity reminds me of the spring when we tore down the old barn and removed the maternity ward of the barn cats. Shortly thereafter I thought I heard kittens crying up in the maple tree, back of the house. Family reaction was that I was "hearing things," but when Man and Boy got a ladder and climbed up to inspect the situation, they found a batch of newborn kittens in an old bucket that had somehow gotten lodged in the big tree. A few days later I heard kitten voices again, this time in the big maple tree in front of the house. Would you believe another bucket? More kittens!

Since then, we have found no more buckets, nor kittens in the trees. But who knows what will turn up? It's spring!

Easter Ham and Eggs

"Welcome, happy morning!" age to age shall say . . .
                                                                —Easter hymn

EVEN after the youngsters no longer believed the Easter Bunny laid those colored eggs, and in fact helped dye and decorate the eggs themselves, I still kept a few surprises up my sleeve. It took them a long time to figure out how once in a while an egg would come out of the dye bath with the person's name appearing on it, like magic. (Perhaps it was a bit sneaky for me to take the wax pencil out of the coloring kit and write a name on a warm egg before passing it along to be dyed, but I'm all for preserving a few illusions, where possible, and their surprise and delight was something to see.) Another surprise was the golden goose egg that would be hidden separately somewhere among the flowers. For a while there they thought we had a special Easter Bunny at our place, one that laid a single golden egg. None of their friends ever found a golden Easter egg.

With many people, ham is the traditional main dish for Easter dinner, and if you live in Maryland it will probably be Stuffed Ham. Thought to have been originated by the early settlers, the idea was more probably brought over from England, where stuffed chine, made exactly the same way, was an even older and earlier traditional dish. One old recipe explains that this method of cooking ham for Easter came into usage because it was considered "imprudent to eat too greatly of fat meats following the fast of Lent."

Where, when, or how the idea started, everyone who has eaten STUFFED HAM agrees it is in a culinary class of its own. The "stuffing" consists of leafy greens, fresh herbs, some member of the onion family, and seasonings of celery seed and black and red pepper. The ham should be sugar cured, lightly smoked, about 6 months in age, and around 12 pounds in size. (In tracking down various recipes I came across one that started "take one canned ham," but I stopped reading right there.)

Once the ham has been soaked overnight and scrubbed it should be covered with cold water, slowly brought to a simmer, and cooked for 1 hour. (In boiling any ham you don't actually boil it; just keep the heat high enough to make the surface of broth shiver slightly.) Then remove the ham from the broth and place it on a large platter, where it can be prepared for stuffing. While it is getting cool enough to handle, wash and drain the leafy greens—at least 1 peck of fresh kale, spinach, mustard greens, "creasies," or turnip greens, or a combination of two or more. Remove thick ribs or stems and chop the leaves. Add about 1 quart of finely chopped parsley and about 2 C chopped shallots, chives, or scallions. Sprinkle with 1 tsp each celery seed, crushed red pepper, coarsely ground black pepper, and coarse salt. Moisten with hot ham broth and mix all together thoroughly. Taste for seasoning and make additions if necessary.

Either make deep slits in ham with a sharp knife or make holes through it lengthwise with a round steel. Pack stuffing into all slits, or holes, and "fold ham in a stout cloth and sew fast." Some recipes call for wrapping and sewing the ham in a piece of heavy linen, but few households can provide heavy linen for wrapping hams these days. A piece of muslin or worn sheet will serve the purpose admirably.

Return the wrapped ham to the kettle of broth, bring back to a simmer, and cook for 15 minutes per pound of ham. At the end of the cooking time remove kettle from heat and allow to cool; then lift the ham from the broth, drain, and chill for at least a day before removing cloth and slicing.

A scaled-down version of Stuffed Ham would be just as good, starting with a smoked picnic or a boneless butt, with smaller amounts of greens, herbs, and seasonings in proportion but following the same general rules for stuffing and cooking.

Wherever there is ham there *should* be biscuits: Buttermilk Biscuits (page 44) in a pinch but preferably BEATEN BISCUITS, the main ingredient of which is elbow grease—that is, unless you happen to be lucky enough to have a biscuit machine. I know of some people who use an old clothes wringer for rolling the dough. I have even considered trying to substitute a pasta machine. But to date my method has depended on a heavy wooden whomper (bought at a sale years ago) and a strong right arm. Since my elbow has developed some type of "-itis" (tendon-, burs-, arthr-) or just plain old rheumatism, we haven't had beaten biscuits as often as I would like them.

If you have the strength, some type of machine, or someone else to do the beating, here's how it goes. Work 1 C cold lard and 2 tsp coarse salt into 8 C flour until texture is mealy. Add just enough ice water to make a very stiff dough. One old recipe suggests "beat with a club." If you don't have a club handy you might try a rolling pin, baseball bat, or any other wooden object that can deliver a telling blow. In any case, beat the dough until blisters are raised (either on the dough or your hands, or both). Roll out dough about ½ inch thick, cut into small rounds, "stick four times with a silver fork," and bake on ungreased pan about 20 minutes at 400°.

What to go with the ham and biscuits? For first choice I'd take SOUTHERN CANDIED TOMATOES. To 2 quarts home-canned tomatoes to which salt has been added before processing add 1½ C brown sugar, ¼ pound butter, and some freshly ground pepper. Cook uncovered on top of stove until it begins to thicken. Stir in about 1 C crisp croutons, put in hot oven, and bake until thick.

For a second vegetable, another non-green one seems best, since there are already greens and herbs in the ham. Something creamy might round out the textural interest of the meal—say, dried corn pudding or cauliflower custard.

For DRIED CORN PUDDING cover 1 C dried corn with 3 C hot milk and add 2 T butter, 1 tsp salt, and 2 T sugar. Stir and set aside to cool. When cool, add 2 well-beaten eggs and mix thoroughly. Pour into buttered baking dish and bake about 50 minutes at 375°.

For the CAULIFLOWER CUSTARD, break 1 large head of cauliflower into florets, cover with boiling water, and cook until just tender. Drain, chop fairly fine, and add 1 T butter and 1 tsp salt. Beat together 2 eggs and 2 C rich milk or thin cream, add to cauliflower mixture, pour into buttered baking dish, set into a shallow pan of hot water, and bake at 350° until firm.

Hard-boiled eggs are usually not a popular item on the menu for Easter, but if the bunny has brought a good supply of them, they can be stored in the refrigerator and recycled in meals the following days. Eggs in Snow (page 41) is an especially good way to use them.

DEVILED EGGS are good alone or with just about anything else. I never make these the same way two times running, but usually some butter, mayonnaise, and mustard is first blended with the mashed yolks. I start the seasonings with salt and pepper and go on to include some kind of spicy sauce, perhaps some aromatic seeds, onion or chives, green peppercorns or capers, and herbs. Additions are made after tasting and deciding what each particular combination needs to round out the flavor.

CURRIED EGGS are good with rice and chutney. When sliced, combined with pimiento and mushrooms, and flavored with sherry, EGGS IN PATTY SHELLS are very good, with green peas on the side. EGGS quartered or left whole can be heated IN CHEESE SAUCE. All three of these start with a basic cream sauce, preferably made with cream; then add desired flavor—curry powder, sherry, or cheese—to taste.

Jim's aunt, Miss Aunt Carrie, used to make a delicious EASTER EGG CASSEROLE the day after. In a buttered baking dish place alternate layers of sliced hard-cooked eggs, sliced parboiled onions, and drained asparagus tips and cut pieces. Cover with a rich cream sauce that has been seasoned with salt, pepper, and grated nutmeg. Top with crumbs and bake at 350°.

The Dandy Dandelion

'Twas with this homely sallet the good wife Hecate entertained Theseus.
— *John Evelyn, 1699*

FROM Greek gods to mere mortals, ancients and moderns, the dandelion has been a dandy source of healing virtues, a tonic for the appetite. The leaves are exceptionally high in vitamin C. The flowers make a soothing tea or a potent "wine." The roasted roots can be combined with coffee or used as a substitute; those long roots go deep into the soil to bring up trace elements and make them available. It ranks first in the list of traditional "bitter" herbs (including endive, chicory, lettuce, and sorrel) eaten with the Passover lamb and is the most important addition to that country dish, a "set of greens."

Call it by any name: *Taraxacum officinale, dent de lion,* or dandelion, but call it good. Only the fanatic lawn freak who resents the invasion of any other living plant in a dull expanse of green grass calls down curses on its head. (To get rid of it he also has to grub it out, root and limb, or destroy every trace of the plants with weed killer.)

The best thing that can be said for eradicating dandelion is that it provides good, healthy outdoor exercise, year after year, without making much of a dent in the dandelion population. Even if every downy head of seed could be removed and destroyed it would make no difference. This is one of the plants that can reproduce itself parthenogenetically, which is a long way of saying it can form tiny unseen buds on the roots, which form seeds without fertilization. And if you get rid of every plant in *your* lawn, the seeds to produce new plants will come in from every direction, from nearby lawns or distant fields, and each one has such a will to grow it can produce plants in the soil-filled cracks of city pavements.

It is much better to just accept the fact that the dandelion is with us, and here it means to stay. Enjoy the beauty of its flowers—if it were rare there would be a rush to get the plants for our gardens—and use the whole plant in the many interesting and flavorful ways that are possible.

The first thing to do is to make some DANDELION TEA, said to be soothing. This will calm down your anti-dandelion fevers. To make the tea, pour 2 C boiling water over 1 C dandelion flowers, allow to steep for about 10 minutes, strain, and drink, slightly sweetened with honey.

For something stimulating rather than soothing, make DANDELION WINE, which is more of a potent liqueur than a wine in the usual sense. If you think this is a mild, bland concoction, brewed and consumed by little old ladies who never "take" spirits, forget it. A couple of years ago I went by to see my friend Azeele one late Sunday morning. In gathering her belongings before moving south, she had come across a bottle of dandelion wine put down about twenty-five years ago. She suggested that I try a sample and I obliged. It looked innocent enough, sort of like liquid sunshine. It went down smooth as silk. Then it hit bottom like a mild explosion—and shortly thereafter I felt a warm glow, all over. The only comparable effect I could remember was when I made a mistake and put 150-proof rum in the eggnog! It could be just the thing to have on hand, for when one feels peckish.

If you want to experiment with a small amount as a trial run, gather ½ gallon of dandelion flowers, cover with 1 gallon of water, bring to boil, and let simmer for about ½ hour. While this is bubbling along, pare thin strips of the rind of 3 lemons and store in a plastic bag in the refrigerator for later use. Add the strained juice of the lemons to 4 pounds of brown sugar, to which the hot strained dandelion juice is also added. (A large crock or enamel kettle is the best thing to make it in.) Stir until sugar is dissolved and mixture is lukewarm. On top of the liquid float a small piece of toast on which you have spread ½ cake of fresh yeast.

Cover and allow to ferment 3 or 4 days, skim off the yeast and toast, strain into bottles, adding some of the lemon peel to each, add bottle tops or corks, and put aside to age. Don't wait twenty-five years to drink it, but do give it a few months' resting time.

For a HOMELY SALLET, cut fresh young dandelion leaves, wash, chill, and serve with a good oil-vinegar dressing. Or follow your usual recipe for wilted lettuce, substituting dandelion leaves for all or part of the lettuce. I usually follow this general procedure. Fill a large salad bowl with fresh crisp dandelion leaves, over which you have chopped 1 hard-boiled egg and a couple of scallions (green tops and all). Dice 2 slices of bacon, cook over slow heat until fat is rendered, and drain the crisp bacon bits on paper. Discarding all but 2 T of the hot bacon fat in the pan, add salt, freshly ground pepper, celery seed, a pinch of sugar, and about 4 T vinegar. Let come to a boil and pour over greens while hot. Toss salad and serve immediately, topped with the crisp bacon bits.

Cooked DANDELION GREENS make a tasty dish, either alone or with other potherbs. A piece of salt pork can be included during cooking, and the vinegar shaker should be at hand for a dash of seasoning if desired.

If there is a comparable term for a congregation of turtles (such as a pride of lions, covey of quail, or flock of sheep) I don't know what it is, but whatever this ingathering is called we have one. We had been keeping a close watch on the island in the pond, waiting for the goose eggs to hatch. Sunday, Jim came rushing in to get the binoculars. *Something* was going on at the east end of the island.

What-thing turned out to be an awe-inspiring invasion of turtles. Or could they be called an invasion if they came from the bottom of the pond? In any case he counted twenty-three in all, crawling on the island, sunning themselves on a half-submerged log—some even coming out on the bank by the dam. We think they aren't snappers; we hope they aren't. We also hope they haven't made away with one of the pair of wood ducks that have taken up residence around the pond. And we'll surely be relieved if and when those goslings come off the nest, intact, and remain that way once they take to water. We hadn't even gone fishing for fear of disturbing that sitting goose. Now we'd like to start reeling in some fish, and we're in the market for advice on turtle-catching too.

Good Breads

"A loaf of bread," the Walrus said,
"Is what we chiefly need."
—Lewis Carroll

GOOD honest bread. Is there anything that smells better while it is baking, or tastes better when it comes from the oven? A loaf of homemade bread can turn an ordinary meal into a feast—or be a meal in itself. White, rye, whole wheat, pumpernickel, French, salt-rising, anadama: the list goes on and on. Each has a distinctive taste and texture; all are worth making from time to time, if not on a regular basis.

And not only does it smell and taste good, baking your own bread can be such a rewarding form of occupational therapy. Punching and kneading dough is a fine way to work off your frustrations and get rid of your aggressions. There are special pails used for mixing large batches of dough, and they're definitely worth investing in if you're making a number of loaves of the same type on a regular basis. Most electric mixers now come with a dough hook, and I frequently use it when I'm pressed for time or having trouble with the "-itis" in my elbow. But I prefer to mix and knead by hand, because only by feel can you tell when dough is perfectly smooth and elastic.

Since flours vary so in density and ability to absorb liquid, I start with the recommended amount of liquid and add flour to make dough of the desired consistency. It is very easy to knead in additional flour, difficult to add more liquid to a dough that is too stiff. Water or potato water will make a loaf with crisp crust. For a smoother crust and softer texture, milk should be used.

For all baking with yeast I use the active dry yeast, available at health food stores, buy it in quantity, and keep it stored in the refrigerator. I buy white or unbleached flour in large bags and store it in a covered stone crock in the pantry. Other flours—rye, whole wheat—and meals—soy, corn, oat, etc.—I buy in smaller quantities, bag up (2 cups to a small plastic bag), and place bags of each type in larger plastic bags in the freezer. This prevents getting the little "wigglies" that like to live in whole-grain flour and meal, and it's very handy to just dip in and get the amount I need of what I want to use.

QUICK CRUSTY BREAD is put together rapidly (I have timed it at about 2 hours from start to finish) and is best when sliced and served warm from the oven, with plenty of fresh sweet butter on the side: good thick slices, that is, that can be used to sop up the juice from a crock of baked soybeans, a mixed casserole of garden-fresh vegetables, or a thick grilled steak.

In a large warm mixing bowl combine ½ C water, warm to the touch, 4 T active dry yeast, and 2 T brown sugar. (To get the mixing bowl warm, pour in some boiling water, swish it around, and pour it out.) When the yeast mixture starts to work, which will be a matter of minutes, add 1½ C lukewarm water and 1 T coarse salt, stir, and add white or unbleached flour, about a cupful at a time, stirring constantly until you have a dough stiff enough to turn out on a floured board. Knead well, adding flour as necessary to keep dough from sticking to board. When ball of dough is smooth and elastic, put it in a *warm* well-greased bowl and cover with a warm damp towel.

Let rise until double in bulk, turn out on floured board, cut dough in half, and shape each piece in a long loaf that will fit on a baking sheet, which has been greased and dusted with dry cornmeal. While dough is "resting," just 5 minutes, place a large shallow pan, half filled with boiling water, on bottom rack of cold oven. Place the baking rack a few inches above it, put pan of bread on the baking rack, close door, and *then* set the oven at 400°. Just put your mind on other things for the next 45 minutes and don't peek in the oven. Be careful about the steam when you open the oven door, and pull out a pan with two of the crispest, crustiest loaves you've ever baked. (Remember, the pan of boiling water and the pan of bread go in a *cold* oven, don't be tempted to peek during the baking period, and keep out of the way of all that steam when you do open the oven door.)

A good CHEWY RYE BREAD takes a little longer but isn't much more trouble to make. Peel and quarter 2 medium-size potatoes. Cover with 2 C water and boil until potatoes are soft. Lift out potatoes, put in a large mixing bowl, and mash thoroughly. Measure potato water and add enough water to make 2 C. Dissolve 3 T active dry yeast in ½ C warm potato water with 1 T molasses or brown sugar. While yeast is beginning to work, add the following to the mashed potato in the large bowl: 1½ C potato water and 1 T each coarse or kosher salt, caraway seed, and bacon grease. Mix thoroughly, add foaming yeast, and stir in 4 C rye flour. When this is thoroughly mixed start adding white or unbleached flour, enough to make a dough that is stiff enough to be handled.

Knead dough on a board that has been dusted with cornmeal (instead of flour), until it is smooth and elastic. Place ball of dough in warm greased bowl, cover with damp cloth, and set aside to rise until doubled in bulk. When dough has risen turn out on board, divide into four parts, form each into an oval-shaped loaf, place on greased baking sheet that has been dusted with cornmeal, let rise until doubled in size, and bake in oven preheated to 375° for about 1 hour. Brush tops of hot loaves with butter, lard, or water.

(Note: To make a less dark bread use just 2 C rye flour and add more of the unbleached or white. If you would like to try a sourdough rye, take 1 C of the dough, before kneading, put it in a covered crock or glass jar, and set aside in a warm place until it starts fermenting. One-half C of this "starter" can replace yeast in the above recipe. It can be stored in refrigerator and kept "going" like any other sourdough starter.)

For regular SOURDOUGH BREAD it may take 5 to

6 days before your starter is ready to use, but from then on —if you keep it properly stored and replenished—it will last for years. To make the starter, put 1 C milk in a glass jar or small crock and let it stand out in room temperature for 24 hours. Stir in 1 C flour, cover with a cloth, and keep in warm place until it is bubbling and working well; this may take anywhere from 2 to 5 days. It may now be used immediately or stored in the refrigerator. When you remove any starter from the jar, replace the amount taken out with some flour mixed with water. To keep the starter jar going, it must have some of the contents removed and replaced with fresh flour and water at least once a week.

To make basic sourdough bread, combine in mixing bowl 1 C starter with 2½ C warm water and 5 C flour. Beat well, cover bowl, and keep at room temperature about 24 hours. Add 1½ tsp soda, 1 T salt, 2 T sugar, 3 T melted butter, and 1 C flour. Mix together and then turn out on a floured board and knead until smooth and shiny, adding flour as necessary to keep dough from sticking. Divide into 2 long loaves, place on greased baking tin that has been sprinkled with cornmeal, let rise until nearly doubled in bulk, and then bake about 45 minutes at 400°. (Instead of a baking sheet I sometimes bake this bread in heavy-gauge steel French bread pans.)

A lot of different breads, rolls, and pancakes can be made with this starter. With it our daughter Tam regularly makes ENGLISH MUFFINS, split while warm, put under the broiler to brown, then drenched with sweet butter. The night before you plan to have the muffins, mix together ½ C starter, 1 C milk, and 2 C flour. This is covered and set in a warm place. The next morning combine ½ C flour, ½ tsp soda, 1 tsp coarse salt, and 1 T sugar and sift the mixture over the dough. Stir this in, turn the dough out on a floured board, and knead lightly until dough is not sticky. Roll out ¾ inch thick, cut into large rounds (a tuna-fish tin with both ends removed makes an excellent cutter), place on a board or pan that has been sprinkled with cornmeal, and sprinkle more cornmeal on top of the muffins. Let these rest for about 15 minutes. To bake them Tam uses a large iron skillet on medium heat, slips the muffins from board to skillet with a pancake turner, and bakes them until they are golden brown on both sides. An electric frypan turns out excellent, evenly browned muffins, set at 275°.

FRENCH BREAD requires the fewest of ingredients, and in some cases the most involved of procedures. I've tried them all but always go back to the first method I used, in the days when French bread and bread sticks just weren't to be had back in the boondocks.

Dissolve 2 T yeast in ¼ C warm water, add ¾ C flour, stir, and knead this small ball of dough until it is smooth. Make a couple of cuts across the top of dough ball and drop it into a bowl containing 2 C warm water. Cover and set aside until dough ball has risen to top of water and formed a light, puffy sponge. Then add 1 tsp salt and stir in enough flour to make a dough stiff enough to knead. Knead dough on floured board until it is smooth and elastic. Place in lightly greased bowl, cover, and let rise until doubled in bulk.

Form long thin loaves or sticks, place on greased baking sheet that has been dusted with cornmeal, let rise again, and bake, about 40 minutes, at 375°. Just before they are done, brush tops and sides of loaves with beaten egg white and return to oven to dry the glaze.

Like Quick Crusty Bread, French Bread can be baked over a shallow pan of hot water to give a crisper crust. French Bread should be concave rather than convex in shape. To get this effect press a narrow furrow along the center of the loaf with the edge of your hand or a piece of round stick after the loaf has been placed in the baking pan. Before baking cut 3 or 4 slashes across the top of the loaf. Recently, some special pans for baking French Bread have come on the market. The one I like best is the heavy-gauge black-steel type.

The type of bread most frequently baked is probably what we call a HOUSEHOLD LOAF, the daily bread made with yeast, baked in loaf pans, and used for everything from breakfast toast to sandwiches. The basic proportions, for two 5-by-10-inch loaves, are 2 C liquid to 2 T each shortening and yeast (or 1 cake of compressed yeast). Some recipes also call for 2 T sugar, but I only use 1 tsp of sugar to start the yeast working. For the above amount use 1 T salt and enough flour to make a workable dough.

Start yeast in ¼ C warm water; the remaining 1¾ C of liquid may be water, milk, or potato water. In a large bowl put shortening (butter, lard, margarine, vegetable oil, or whatever), salt, and sugar (if used) and cover with warm liquid. Add yeast mixture and enough flour to make a batter.

This first stage will take about 2 C flour, which can be regular white or unbleached, whole wheat, graham, or rye. Or, to vary the flavor and texture, you can substitute ⅓ C wheat germ for the same amount of flour; 1 C soy flour or cornmeal to replace the same amount of white flour; or use ½ C each cornmeal, rye flour, whole wheat, and white flour. Or add 2 C rolled oats to liquids, plus enough flour to make batter. If you want to increase the nutritive value, add ½ C dry skim milk at this stage.

When the batter is smooth, stir in enough additional white or unbleached flour to make a dough that can be turned out on a floured board and kneaded until it is smooth and elastic. Place the ball of dough in a greased bowl, cover with a damp cloth, and allow to rise in a warm place until double in bulk.

When the dough has risen turn it out on the board, divide it into two loaves, place them in greased pans, and set aside to rise again. *Or*, before making into loaves add and work in 1 C raisins or shredded cheese, or ½ C onions cooked until soft in a bit of butter, or 1 C sprouted wheat. (Aromatic seeds or herbs can also be incorporated into the dough at this stage.)

When the pans of bread have risen to double bulk, bake in preheated 450° oven 10 minutes, reduce the heat to 350°, and continue baking until the loaves shrink from the sides of the pans. About 40 minutes' baking time in all is about right. After 30 minutes I turn the bread loaves out of the pan and finish baking them on the oven racks, which gives a crisper crust.

When bread is done, brush the tops with butter and cool the loaves on a wire rack. Of course there's no law that says you can't slice it while it is warm from the oven and spread with fresh sweet butter. The slices won't be neat, but who cares about tidy slices when the flavor and aroma are so wonderful?

The other day, by chance, I turned out some loaves that had much the flavor and texture of salt-rising bread, but they were a whole heap easier to make. For breakfast we had had corn cakes, made with buttermilk and soda. About a cup of batter was left over, so I dumped it in the bread bowl along with the liquid, salt, and butter, decreasing liquid to 1½ C in all. From here on I used the usual white-bread routine. It was so good I'm going to try a version that uses cornmeal, buttermilk, and soda from scratch and see if I get the same effect.

MAY
Of Herbs and Other Country Messes

> ... *now sing*
> *Of herbs, and other country messes,*
> *Which the neat-handed Phyllis dresses.*
> —Milton, L'Allegro

MANY country people call them "yarbs." The French call them "airbs." You may call them "urbs." My preferred pronounciation (unless you habitually drop your aitches, as in 'eaven, 'ell, and 'enry) is herbs, with an *h*. But by any name, nothing beats a good mess of greens, or wild potherbs, for waking up the taste buds, serving as a spring tonic, and stretching the food budget. Some are native plants; others were brought to this country by the colonists but have long since escaped to roadsides and pastures. All abound at this season and are to be had for the picking or gathering.

Perhaps the best known and most frequently used is the upland or winter cress—"creasies" or "creasy greens." If you catch the plants while the rosettes of leaves are young, they make a delicious salad, either alone or combined with other leafy vegetables and prepared like dandelion greens.

Later, when the cress is more abundant, it can be cooked in a number of ways. If you're exploring the delights of stir-fry cookery, try this method with cress, using a small amount of peanut oil and then flavoring with a dash of good soy sauce. A different but equally good cooking method is to steam the freshly washed leaves—without adding any extra water—for just a few minutes and then season with salt, pepper, and butter. *And* a big pot of creasies, cooked longer, with more water and a chunk of fatback—and plenty of hot skillet cornbread to sop up the pot likker—is not to be despised.

Still later in the season, when the leaves have gotten bitter, there is another crop to be gathered, the young flowering stems. If these are gathered while still in bud, steamed, and then served with melted butter and seasoning, they're infinitely better than the tame and frequently tired asparagus and broccoli we find in the supermarket.

There are a lot of other good potherbs: sheep's sorrel, lamb's quarters, mustard (both black and white), pigweed, poke (be careful to collect just the newly emerged shoots; the roots and older leaves are toxic), and, of course, the ubiquitous dandelion. Some people like to combine a mixture of several or all of these. Each time they are served there will be a subtle difference in flavor, depending on how much of each plant is included.

The various types of wild onions and garlic shouldn't be overlooked, either. Some are so mild and sweet they can be used raw or in cooking generally. The tender tops of any of them can be chopped and added to salads or sandwich spreads. Most of them are good in highly seasoned foods like spaghetti sauce or tacos.

There is one member of the onion tribe that is in a class by itself, and to say that it is a cultivated taste is a masterpiece of understatement. This is the wild leek or "ramp." Ramps grow in moist woods, usually in mountain areas. People who are real ramp buffs can and do travel miles to indulge a craving for this really wild way-out flavor. There is even an annual Ramp Festival in West Virginia, and ramp freaks from all over make the trek to attend and participate in this Rite of Spring. They are never accompanied by wives, seldom by children, and are always urged to remain away from home for days or weeks afterward—until the last vestiges of ramp scent have faded from the breath and stopped exuding through the pores.

Just hauling a bunch of ramps in the back end of an automobile is said to make it unfit for further human use. In fact, should you ever get downwind of a colony, there is no danger of confusing it with anything else known to man.

The Young Gardener

But though an old man, I am but a young gardener.
—Thomas Jefferson, 1811

THE "young" gardener I have in mind is not the child who first explores the mystery of poking a seed into the earth but rather the person who may be long in the tooth, creaking in the joints, with failing back and aching muscles, but who still has a sense of wonder and a lively curiosity about the green and growing world. Hardly a minute, much less a day, goes by that we can't see something we never noticed before, or learn something new. So much is going on it just isn't possible to take it all in. Every time I look out a window or go outside the door there is something fascinating and different to see.

One day I spent far too much time watching a bumblebee "work" the flowers of a patch of shooting star, just outside the sliding glass doors in the living room. (Time, I might add, that should have been spent dusting the furniture and sorting out the mountain of papers on the gateleg table. Oh, well, the dust and papers will stay there until I get around to them and, meanwhile, what a diverting sight!) The flower stems are thin and frail and don't provide a good foothold for something as big and heavy as a bumblebee, but the bee was determined and the operation was successful. Now every stem is topped with swelling pods of forming seeds.

From the windows in the sewing room I watched another performance that kept me from doing more mundane things. There is a patch of bright blue Ajuga that comes back year after year, along with some creamy orange tulips (de Wet by name) and clumps of lords-and-ladies (*Narcissus bifloris*) and snowflakes (*Leucojum*). I had seen an occasional oriole or two, and frequently there are finches flying about, but here was a convention: Baltimore orioles, orchard orioles, goldfinches—male and female, old and young—feasting on the lower buds of the spikes of Ajuga flowers. A beautiful sight, and a "first" in my experience; I never realized that these birds were attracted by this plant.

Another first, but not as delightful, is the discovery that the wild rabbits are even eating the tops of green onions out in the garden. With acres of wild onion and garlic on the outside of the garden fence, why do they have to make the effort to come in and devour my Riverside Sweet Spanish onions, raised from seed?

While inspecting the onion damage I made another decidedly unpleasant discovery: dodder on the onion plants. Dodder is called a number of names, few of them flattering—strangleweed, devil's-hair, pull-down, hell-bind, to mention a few. It starts from a seed; then, as soon as the thin yellow or orange threads latch onto another plant, the root dies and from then on the dodder lives on the host plant, climbing and spreading and eventually forming a matted tangle that destroys the host. The only way to control it is to remove every single bit of the vine and burn it—or apply the pre-emergent weed killer Dacthal before it appears.

Another less than charming sight I am seeing right now is the swelling population of aphids. There are a great many species, injurious to all forms of vegetation. Don't be misled by the old wives' tale that onions or garlic will keep away aphids. We have forty acres of wild onion and garlic and all kinds and colors of aphids: green, yellow, black, brown, gray, red, blue, white. The only way to control them is by applying a contact insecticide when they appear; nicotine sulfate (Black Leaf 40), Malathion, and Thiodan are all effective. *In using any spray material carefully read and follow exactly all instructions on the label.* Some labels do not give instructions for mixing small lots of spray, so be sure to figure out the right proportions of spray to water if they aren't already listed. (For instance, since 1 quart of Thiodan should be mixed with 100 gallons of water, in small amounts this works out to 1 tablespoon Thiodan to 1½ gallons of water.)

Our pleasure in the geese and goslings was intense but brief. On the morning of May Day, I looked down at the pond and saw the new goslings launched: a flotilla of six bobbing bits of fluff, with the proud mama and papa floating fore and aft. For several days we were diverted by their antics; then for some reason they moved on. They may have left because of the turtles, or because we changed the environment by mowing around the pond. Jim managed to drive them back from the middle of Route 7 one time, but we just gave up when they wandered off in another direction.

On the subject of turtles, one reader had a good suggestion for catching snappers. I don't doubt I could catch them, but I'm afraid the system would break down when it came to the stage of "dispose or relocate." Disposing of or relocating snapping turtles doesn't fall within my range of skills or interests!

Something new in the garden this season: I tried transplanting snap beans which had been started in the greenhouse, and it works. Yesterday for lunch I enjoyed a sneak preview of good things to come—a small serving of beans, fresh from the garden. So far the rabbits are the only ones who are enjoying the garden peas, and if they continue at the present rate there won't be any for the rest of us.

One thing that nothing seems to bother is the sweet

rocket or dame's violet (*Hesperis matronalis*), now in full bloom. Native from southern Europe to Siberia, this is one of the plants brought to this country by the early settlers which escaped from gardens and has naturalized in a number of areas. It is really handsome, growing up to 3 feet, topped with clusters of phloxlike flowers that are white, lavender, or rose pink, with a sweet scent during the evening and night hours. Good in the garden, it is also nice to use in arrangements.

As of last week we have something new on the place that is going to either make me feel younger or much older. I am now owned by an Alaskan Malamute named Chaka, at least as big as I am and about five times as strong. It may take her a little while to get me trained, but it is already apparent that she has the will and she will doubtless find the way. Unlike most of the other dogs we have had (which could all be classed as canine garbage disposals), she is a picky eater. So far the only bribe to which she responds is one of my homemade chocolate cookies, and she doesn't listen when I explain that we can't build a lasting relationship on the basis of a one-way cookie exchange.

Apples of Love and Bean Poles

Apples of Love are very much used in Italy to putt when Ripe into their Brooths & soops giving it a pretty Tart Taste. A lady Just come from Leghorn sayes She thinks it gives an Agreeable Tartness & Relish to them & she Likes it Much.
—Letter from Peter Collinson to
John Custis, February, 1742

WHILE Jefferson was the first to record notes on tomato growing in Virginia, in 1781, the Collinson letters indicate that Custis was interested in them forty years earlier. My guess is that they were first grown by Custis in the early 1740s.

In any case, we have been growing and enjoying the "pretty Tart Taste" of love apples or tamiatas for a long, long time, and it is the vegetable grown by the most people today. Even a single plant growing in a large container on the terrace will produce quantities of ripe fruit for salads; half a dozen plants well grown in the flower border will supply enough fresh fruits for any average family.

We have forty fine plants, carefully "caged," well mulched, and full of tomatoes, some of which should be ripe at least by July Fourth. Next week I plan to set out more, for another main crop to come along later and provide plenty of green tomatoes for relish, pickles, frying, and freezing.

When we first moved to Loudoun County, August 1 nearly thirty years ago, one thing we had to leave behind was a handsome tomato patch just coming into full production. I brought along a few of the side shoots, or suckers, dipped them in Rootone, stuck them in the ground, and we had a dandy crop of tomatoes later on. Other years since then I have just started out with half a dozen plants, rooting suckers in succession for several weeks. This is a good idea, for it keeps a fresh crop coming along throughout the season and avoids the usual inundation of ripe tomatoes that have to be dealt with at any one time.

We are growing five varieties: Golden Ponderosa, the biggest and best yellow type; Ponderosa, the old favorite, still tops for flavor; Ultra Boy, supposed to be the best of the "boy" types; Veeroma, a much improved Italian type; and a Japanese hybrid, super quality for slicing and salads. Before planting, holes were prepared by adding some compost, rotted manure, greensand, and rock phosphate. After planting, each plant was side dressed with one tablespoon of Epsom salts and half a cup of 5–10–10, well watered in.

While debating the subject of what to use for "cages," marauders (either groundhogs or rabbits) did some unplanned pruning of the plants. After consultation with Ed Nichols of Nichols Hardware, I came to the quick decision to use concrete reinforcing wire. At the same time we had consultations on what to use to support pole or

Apples of Love and Bean Poles / 95

climbing beans. (We have plenty of prospective poles on the place—native cedars of just the right size—but the Resident Woodsman had the best possible excuse for not cutting them: his ax needs a new handle.)

But back to the pole discussion, during which Asa Moore Janney, the Squire of Downtown Lincoln, came in, looking very stylish, I might add, wearing a Southern Planter's hat. "Asey" Moore's solution to the problem was not to plant pole beans at all but to plant bush varieties and give them plenty of phosphate and potash! (As I told him at the time, this is a typical answer to a problem when one doesn't know the answer.)

A few days later I still had all that pole bean seed and no poles when we went to a party and saw Tom Taylor, the Sage of North Fork. Other people may have been discussing world-shaking subjects, but bean poles were on my mind. Praises be, Tom had the solution—a barn loft full of bamboo poles he had been saving for "something" for at least fifteen years. At his invitation we went up early the next morning and loaded the luggage rack of our little wagon with long bamboo poles. It looked like a little grass shack on wheels and caused a great deal of interest and some comment. One motorist did a doubletake, slammed on his brakes, came over to the car, and, peering through the window, asked, "Goin' fishin'?" Jim took another draw on his pipe, puffed out the smoke, then said, "Well, I *might*."

The poles are in place, the beans are planted. Now all I have to do is figure out some way to keep the wild critters from eating them as soon as they come up. So far, the rabbits and groundhogs have finished off five small patches of peas, topped most of the bush beans, and are now started on the cabbage and purple cauliflower plants. To date I've tried everything, including moth balls, dried blood, rock phosphate, lime, and various spray materials, and nothing has had the desired effect. Jack Brown, the County Agent, tells me that nothing will prevent this damage except a physical barrier, such as a fence.

Well, I've already got a fence around the whole garden, and all it does, apparently, is provide some healthy exercise for the animals that climb over it or burrow under it. Helps them work up a better appetite for the fresh vegetables growing on the inside.

In desperation, I concocted a witches' brew. After grinding a Jamaican hot pepper, a regular cayenne pepper, and a handful of chile piquin, I added the mixture to water and boiled to extract all the "heat." The strained juice was added to a spray of Sevin and applied liberally to everything that is being consumed before its time. Either this is going to prevent these plants from being eaten or our particular rabbits are going to have the hottest lips in Loudoun County.

The next time I see Ed Nichols I'm going to give him a small piece of my mind. As I recall, for Mother's Day he suggested giving Mom a new stove! Would you believe his suggestions for Father's Day? Chaise longues, hammocks, gliders, wood porch swings, rockers, and recliners.

I had something slightly different in mind, say, *something like a new ax handle.*

JUNE
Gifts for the Bride

*I slept and dreamed that life was beauty;
I woke and found that life was duty.*

—*Anonymous*

FROM around 1850 to the turn of the century, sentiments like the above, embroidered in fancy stitches on pillow shams, dresser scarves, "tidies," or hand-crocheted antimacassars, were not only considered suitable gifts for the bride but *de rigueur* for the well-appointed household in which she would be starting married life.

In the twenties, in England, it was the fashion in smart circles to give the bride and groom separate presents, rather than selecting something they would use together and possibly face an argument over dividing should the need arise.

In this country the custom started of selecting one's patterns of silver, china, and crystal and "registering" the preference with local sources for them, who would in turn urge would-be givers to buy one or more items until the requisite dozen of each had been purchased. (This custom led to the fantasy that a newly married couple had to start out with wall-to-wall everything material, but it did not result in lasting happiness.)

What about today's bride? As surely as the month of June rolls around, a lot of people are going to be wondering what to give her. What does she need? Well, just like the brides of any other age, the things she is going to need the most are those that no one can give her: a sense of wonder, a sense of beauty, certainly a sense of humor, and at least a modicum of that uncommon commodity, common sense.

To get some ideas and suggestions for the material gifts one might select for today's bride, I took an unscientific poll. It covered three generations and several life-styles and the results were interesting if not altogether helpful. First, I asked which wedding gift or gifts had meant the most to each person, excluding substantial items like family silver. The answers ranged all the way from a Queen Anne chair (the real thing, not a reproduction) to a scrap basket (which the owner described as being very pretty and endlessly useful). Some of the more successful gifts were not things the person had a particular need for, but nonetheless they loved getting them and have a special feeling for them. These included some handsome old library steps and some charming afterdinner coffee cups that have butterfly handles.

One person received sixty pairs of sterling silver candlesticks, surely more than any one household could put to good use. Electing to keep only a few of the ones she liked most, she exchanged the others for one large, important piece of silver. Another person was delighted to receive twelve dozen candles which she uses in quantities for special candlelight occasions. A very new and young bride got the greatest pleasure from a single huge candle that will be lit and cast its light for many happy occasions to come. (Made by a young friend of the couple, it took pounds of wax and a lot of time and imagination. A foot square and about eight inches high, it consists of rainbow layers of different soft colors. Definitely unusual and very beautiful.)

Most brides like to receive something old that has pleasant associations for them. One of them mentioned pieces of Canton china that had been in constant use for two or three generations and repaired with rivets when broken, which she continues to use with pleasure. She also has a charming little cream jug and sugar bowl of répoussé silver which she uses every day, and each time it reminds her of the days when they went on family picnics and used the cream and sugar for bowls of fresh strawberries.

A gift that made a hit was a leather-bound dictionary. Leather-bound or not, every household should have a good dictionary that could and *should* be used every day. Several people have used scrapbooks and photograph albums. (In my own case I have a plentiful supply of each but never get around to sticking the suitable items in them!)

Sometimes one is able to pass along a perfect gift that is suitable, beautiful, and will have a unique meaning for the person receiving it. One doting aunt we know was able to give the Portuguese bride of a nephew a length of brocade, long enough to make a dress, which had belonged to a Portuguese princess.

For most of us, most of the time, a wedding gift can't be so grand, but it can be useful and give pleasure. "In my day," said one person, "people gave you what they wanted you to have." I must admit that this is still the case with me. While I hope the bride will enjoy and use a gift I select, I do not go along with the idea of buying a single piece of anything to make up a matched set of something. I operate on the theory that if the bride needs and wants the things that some people look on as necessities—electric toasters, frypans, irons, coffee makers, et cetera, et cetera, et cetera—she'll find a way to get them. Probably most brides of today don't want to be loaded down with a lot of possessions for which they have no desire or use.

Finally, one must consider the sort of life the newly married couple is going to lead. They may start out in anything from a plastic dome in the woods to a high-rise apartment. They may both be going to college or the groom may be employed by a company that shifts employees, regularly, from one coast to the other. Moving and storage costs can make many possessions a real financial burden.

Perhaps the best wedding gifts for today's bride will be those that are not too bulky in size, things that are attractive and useful and not too obviously valuable. Several people I know give a more or less standard gift to every bride. One of these is a simple pewter syrup pitcher on a small pewter plate. It looks well with any pattern of china, requires minimum care, and can be used daily (the pitcher can be filled with flowers if you aren't serving syrup). There are, in fact, numerous pieces of pewter that make good gifts. Jefferson cups are a nice shape and suitable size for serving anything cold to drink (milk, juleps, tea, juice), and anywhere from one to a dozen should please any bride. The miniature version of this cup also makes a nice gift, to be used for cigarettes, as a jigger, for liqueurs, or to hold small flowers.

Any of the enamel-coated iron casseroles that can go from freezer, to oven, to table should be welcome. Even more useful (and I happen to think they are quite good-looking objects) would be cast-iron skillets, cornstick or popover pans, or dutch ovens.

Then there are baskets, which are beautiful and will serve as multipurpose containers. It is still possible to get handsome handwoven sweet-grass baskets from the Carolinas, Indian baskets from the Southwest, oak-splint baskets from the Appalachians, and baskets beautifully woven of various materials from many other countries. In fact, baskets might be the best gift of all for the bride of the seventies—useful, beautiful, portable, requiring little upkeep and no polishing, long-lasting, and available in any price range. They are suitable for use just about anywhere, in any surroundings, even turning up as plant and flower containers at posh embassy receptions.

Finally, here is a gift for every bride, of any age, at any time. Saint-Exupéry said it: Love is not two people standing face to face, but two people facing the same direction, hand in hand. If you have this gift it is amazing how little the material possessions matter; no one can take it away from you. In fact, the more of it you give, the more you have left to keep giving.

The Year of the Rabbit Is Right!

First he ate some lettuces and some French beans; and then he ate some radishes; and then . . . he went to look for some parsley.
—Beatrix Potter, The Tale of Peter Rabbit

THERE must be a point at which one gives up the whole idea of having a vegetable garden, and I must just about have reached it.

The hot-lips formula of pepper juice did *not* work; in fact, it seemed to attract, rather than repel, the rabbits and groundhogs. At least, after it was applied they finished off the first planting of beans (full of blooms and small beans) and looked upon the entire patch of purple cauliflower and cabbage and found it good. Now they're digging the freshly sprouted pole beans and eating them before they get out of the ground! And it shouldn't take them more than another day to consume the last of the lettuce.

The crops harvested to date—a few green onions and radishes and a few leaves of Bibb lettuce—hardly seem like an impressive return on the money, time, and energy invested in this project.

Like the line in the poem I'm "standing with reluctant feet," trying to decide whether to admit complete defeat or go out and plant more seed to produce more succulent delicacies for all the odious animals.

In the Chinese calendar this is the Year of the Rabbit. I believe, *I believe*. It also appears to be the year of the tick and the gnat and, from the number of grubs I've been finding, the year of the beetle. (Gather ye rosebuds while ye may.)

So far, Chaka the Malamute has caught one squirrel and one groundhog. Not a very high batting average considering the numerical strength of the enemy, but at least her presence on and around the front porch seems to discourage the playful antics of the critters that used the hanging baskets like a jungle gym in years past. It would be nice if the new trailing begonias could come through the season without disaster striking. They are the Aphrodite series of the recently developed Rieger begonias, the colors are soft shades of pink, rose, and red, and the trailing plants are a mass of flowers all summer. Truly beautiful.

Another thing that pleasures me right now is the fancy-leaf geraniums. Once the darling of Victorian gardeners, they fell out of favor for some time, but nearly every nursery will stock a few and some growers specialize in them. They're worth tracking down, for the leaves are so varied and interesting in different shades of green, gold, and cream, some with zones of contrasting colors, others splashed with red and bronze or edged with white. One of my favorites is Happy Thoughts, and believe me I can use a lot of happy thoughts these days.

One of them is remembering the day our friend Mary Schoene brought down some fresh strawberries, just picked from her patch up at Waterford. There is nothing better than a fresh, fully ripe strawberry still warm from the sun, a luxury we don't enjoy often. I finally gave up trying to raise our own, because I did all the work and the birds got all the berries. This year, having no strawberries, the birds had to make do with cherries. We have a lot of cherry trees; usually the crop provides enough for us and the birds in addition to a few friends who like to come and pick them. Well, this time the birds took them all, just before they got ripe. It begins to dawn on me that perhaps nature has gotten out of balance around here. It sure seems ridiculous to have at least twenty-five cherry trees without getting a single cherry, much less enough to make a pie or two and put up a few jars of preserves. Could it be possible that the birds and other creatures have spread the word that Great Aunt Jane sets a good table and she's a soft touch?

At the edge of the woods, along the roads, and clustered in fence corners, the elder is in flower. This herb plays an important role in mythology and folklore and is said to have wonderful powers to do just about everything, from removing freckles to protecting one from evil spirits. One of the easiest recipes calling for elder flowers is ELDER VINEGAR. Gather the blossoms and dry them by spreading them on a screen or a frame covered with cheesecloth. Fill a bottle with dried blossoms, cover with white wine vingar, and leave in a warm place for a week or so. Strain and bottle the flavored vinegar, which will have a subtle and interesting aroma and taste.

An old recipe for ELDER FLOWER FRITTERS suggests that flowers should be picked as they are beginning to open, when they have "a very fine smell and a spirited Taste." Break the large fresh flower clusters into small sections, dip in any fritter batter, and deep fry until light brown. Before serving, sprinkle fritters with powdered sugar and grated lemon peel.

Then there is ELDER BLOSSOM TEA, which has a fragrant, refreshing flavor. Pour 3 C boiling water over 1 C fresh elder flowers, add a sprig of mint, and allow the tea to steep for 5 to 10 minutes before serving hot or cold.

ELDER WINE is another of those delicious and deceptive drinks that look and taste mild but have something of a kick. It is made just like Dandelion Wine (page 79).

When I set out a tiny plant of lovage a year ago I thought it would get to be about two feet tall and hoped it would provide enough seeds for me to raise additional plants. Though it is said that it "joyeth to grow in shadowy places and loves running water," it was planted in full sun, in a fairly dry spot. Well, this season it has shot up to over seven feet (dwarfing everything else in that bed) and is now forming enough seed to plant and to use in quantity in seasoning. In some countries they have used lovage seed as a substitute for black pepper. It might make an interesting addition to curry powder.

Lovage may or may not be a good addition to the seasoning shelf, but in any case it makes a handsome border plant. Next time I'll put it at the back of the border! And *then* it won't get over two feet tall.

Wildflowers of Summer

> Ye field flowers! the gardens eclipse you 'tis true;
> Yet wildings of nature, I dote upon you.
> —*Thomas Campbell, "Field Flowers"*

Less than two weeks ago our highways were a glorious sight, lined with miles of lovely flowers: daisies, Queen Anne's lace, chicory, black-eyed Susan, tawny daylilies et al. At the flowers' prime, along came the mowing machines, laying waste to all this beauty, cutting it down to stubble. It happens every year and it should be stopped. Our native plants are already losing an uneven struggle with herbicide spray, the bulldozer blade, and air pollution.

Meanwhile, there are still wildflowers to be found, particularly in spots that are inaccessible to the large mowers, along remote back roads, in fence corners or fields, beside streams, and around ponds. And this is the season when the most and the most varied ones can be seen. Most of the white-flowered types come early in the season, but daisies, Queen Anne's lace, yarrow, and pearly everlasting will continue to bloom until frost. In damp, shaded spots you may find colonies of black snakeroot or cohosh, a tall handsome plant topped with long slender wands of creamy white flowers.

The flowers of meadow rue are inconspicuous, but the ferny, blue-green foliage is lovely—beautiful in arrangements. Jimsonweed or angel's-trumpets can be found in many locations; later the spiky round pods may be collected for dried arrangements.

Perhaps the showiest group of wildflowers includes the yellow-orange-red flowers. In limestone areas, especially, you'll find lots of the great mullein, also called velvet plant and flannel plant. They're striking looking, with tall central stems of pale yellow flowers and large basal leaves of a velvety gray-green. The smaller moth mullein is less showy, but the small, creamy, dark-centered flowers are charming and attract both moths and butterflies.

The brilliant orange butterfly weed is really an eye-stopper; in this area one finds only occasional small clumps. Hard to transplant—but easily grown from seed, collected and planted as soon as ripe—it makes a handsome garden plant.

During the day you may not notice the sundrops or evening primrose, because the pale-yellow fragrant flowers do not open until late afternoon or evening. This is another nice one for the garden, if you have a spot with some moisture and light shade.

On sunny banks you'll find spreading clumps of toadflax, or butter-and-eggs, which look like miniature snapdragons. Also in sunny dry places you're likely to find some of the Saint-John's-wort and rock rose, mostly small shrubs, good for the garden. And along banks, covering brush or buildings, or climbing through high trees there is a lot of trumpet vine in full bloom.

In ponds or streams, look for spatterdock (the yellow pond lily) and water chinquapin (the native yellow lotus). In shady, damp ditches you may find jewelweed. Again, the flowers aren't showy but it is a very useful plant; fresh bruised leaves rubbed on the skin before or after contact with poison ivy will prevent or cure rash.

The list of blue or lavender-flowered plants isn't very long. Other than the many thistles and asters, which seem to thrive anywhere, most of the "blues" are found in damp or marshy places. There is a lot of mistflower (sometimes called wild ageratum), but you really have to search for Lobelia (bright blue), bottle gentian, and monkshood.

More of the wild flowers seen right now are in the pink-rose-red group. Bouncing Bet is bouncing all over the place (also called soapwort because the roots make a foamy-lather soap substitute). The pale to bright pink flowers appear in clusters, like phlox.

Most gardeners shudder at the thought of magenta phlox, but when it escapes from the garden and thrives in a natural setting, nothing could be more handsome. There is one large colony "up the road" I make a special trip to see each summer.

If you have ever traveled the Jersey Turnpike in August, you'll never forget the sight of acres—miles—of rose mallow (the native hardy hibiscus). I have found one colony of it near White's Ferry.

In fields and fencerows you are likely to find a lot of the native spiraeas, both meadowsweet and steeplebush. Then there are the wild roses, and nothing is more delicate and beautiful than some of the small single types. These are usually not found growing in great quantity in any one spot, but over near Waxpool the sweetbrier, or eglantine, is a sight to see—festoons of it hanging from trees and draped over fences and banks. (This is the one that has fragrant foliage and handsome hips, later in the season.)

In marshy spots, the milkweeds abound. The giant types catch your eye from a distance; closer inspection will probably reveal some of the smaller swamp milkweed growing nearby. It has lovely pink to carmine flowers.

Two really red reds are the cardinal flower, found along streams, and bee balm, which also likes a rather moist location. Bee balm, or bergamot, or Oswego tea, makes a delicious herbal tea and is a sure lure for hummingbirds.

The marsh vetchling—sometimes called perennial sweet pea—is not fragrant, but the flowers (white, pink, or purple) are fairly large and of nice form, and the plant has an interesting trailing habit. Very good for arrangements.

Finally, look around you, see what is growing on your own land. Even a tiny yard could spare the space for a few chicory plants, and they're worth having just to see the goldfinches they attract. In our own front field we just discovered for the first time Sabbatia, or marsh pink (doubtless brought in by the birds). The six-petaled flowers are in lovely shades of pink; in the throat is a tiny green star with a faint line of red edging it. A most welcome, if uninvited, visitor.

Some sort of wildflower book is essential, if you want to know more about the ones you find, preferably a handbook that can be taken along when you go "hunting." For the novice there are two companion titles in the Golden Nature Guide Series, *Flowers* and *Weeds*; both are inexpensive paperbacks and when used together they give a good introduction to the world of wildflowers. Once you've gone on beyond being a beginner, there is Peterson's *Field Guide to Wildflowers*.

For sheer delight in reading—and remarkably good descriptions for identification—get the Dover reprints of Mrs. Dana's book on ferns and Frances Parsons's book on wildflowers.

The Third Season

JULY
A Report from the Garden

Good fences are hard to find.
—Great Aunt Jane

LAST week it became obvious that something had to be done about the garden fence. It was *there*, somewhere in a tangle of honeysuckle, poison ivy, and multiflora rose, but it wasn't even slowing down the traffic of rabbits and other raiders and it was so overgrown we couldn't see where they were getting through, or under. The only problem was that getting that fence line cleared using ordinary tools like scythe, sickle, corn knife, machete, and clippers would be a job that could go on into the *next* growing season.

Just in time to save my reason, and possibly the rest of the garden, I heard about a gadget called a Weed Eater and lost no time in contracting to have it make a house call. It came and it conquered.

Now we can see the fence, and it is possible for Chaka to patrol the entire line, which she does frequently. Meanwhile, just to be on the safe side we went ahead and finished making playpens for the pole beans, little wire circles around each cluster of beans. What with these, the tomato cages, and some newly devised supports for cucumbers, the garden is now wired for everything but sound. And it may come to that, too, when the corn begins to ripen and the raccoons come calling.

On June 16 we set some sort of record: took the last jar of tomatoes off the pantry shelf and picked the first ripe tomato from the garden. This reminded me it was high time to get all the herb seeds in the ground to make the best home-processed tomatoes anyone ever ate.

Trisha Cole, who is helping me with the herbs and flowers this summer, watched me planting the parsley seed and expressed doubts as to when, if ever, I would get parsley plants. Parsley is supposed to be difficult to germinate. One of the myths concerning it is the belief that the seed goes to the devil and back nine times before it will sprout. Not so, not so. It takes about 5 days, if you plant fresh seed and handle it the right way. (By *fresh* seed I mean that which is not more than a year or so old.) Pulverize the soil where you want parsley to grow, dampen it if there hasn't been a recent rain, scatter seed in a wide band on top of the soil, and do not cover it with any soil but place a board over it to exclude light and retain moisture. Lift the board every few days to check progress. As soon as the seeds sprout, remove the board and shade the planting with a piece of newspaper for a day or so, if it is hot and dry. The same method works for any other small seeds that have a hard coat.

One vegetable the animals haven't devoured is the beets, and that particular bed looks handsome. It has also given us some of the best eating of the season, tops and all. I pull the beets when they are about 1 inch in diameter, scrub them, cut off roots and about 2 inches of stem and cook for a few minutes, just long enough for the skins to slip off easily. Meanwhile, wash leaves and stems, cut into short lengths, and cover with cold water to keep crisp. Just a few minutes before serving, shift cut leaves and stems and peeled beets to cooking pan, adding just enough water to keep them from burning. Cook until just tender, add kosher salt, freshly ground pepper, and a lump of butter for seasoning, and then serve with some good bread for sopping up the juice.

A Report from the Garden

One of the prettiest things on the place right now is the white waterlilies on the pond. Tired as I am at the end of the day, I have to walk down to the pond, just to see them close up. Nothing could be more restful or beautiful in the evening light. Neither they nor the oriental lotus have required a minute of care since I planted them, and all I did then was wade out in the pond, stick a root of each down in the mud, and cover it with a rock to hold it in place. In return they have given us years of pleasure, summer after summer, and I can't see that they have ever had an adverse effect on the pond. From a practical standpoint they also serve a purpose, providing protection for the small fry as they hatch.

Even if you don't have a pond you can have the pleasure of growing waterlilies in a small tub or container. There are day- and night-blooming types of various soft colors or white. There are at least two miniature varieties, and the size goes on up to dinner-plate diameter. The night-blooming types are especially satisfactory for people who work all day and can only enjoy flowers during the evening hours.

A spot check of the garden this morning shows no additional damage since the fence was cleared. Not that there wasn't enough to go round before! Since I'm too tired to do a rain dance I guess we had better start up the pond pump. This means we have to lay down the pipe, check the wiring, and prime the pump, all of which takes about a day to do. But usually when we get around to doing it, the rains come.

The garden check also shows that all the cucumber seed, planted three days ago, has popped up. These should never look back. After digging fairly deep holes I put in manure and compost before replacing the soil. Then the supports were set in place, circles of wire 4 feet tall and 1 foot in diameter. After watering the circles I stuck in the seeds and covered them with some finely pulverized soil. The wire circles will be kept filled with layers of weeds or grass clippings, with some manure and lime added from time to time. When the plants require water it will be poured down through the circle of composting material. This should give the plants a rich, moist root run, the vines will be trained up on the wire, and the composted weeds will be a plus for the next year's garden. As soon as the plants get going I'll side-dress them with greensand and rock phosphate and add mulch to keep down the weeds.

The peppers are full of buds, the earlier planting of cucumbers is about to start blooming, and the tomatoes are a sight to see—huge plants filled with flowers and fruits. Only the dodder is vile. Can't remember ever seeing so much of it, and it is growing faster than we can uncurl and burn it. Every plant is supposed to have some purpose, but to my knowledge none has been found for dodder. It's a curse, and we have more than our fair share of it.

Garden Raiders Are Persistent Cusses

Whet up your knife and whistle up your dog,
Whet up your knife and whistle up your dog,
We're all goin' huntin', for to catch a groun'hawg
... groun'hawg.

—Folk song

OH, the canniness of these cussed creatures! Chaka just missed patrolling the garden fence line a couple of days, laid up with an injured paw, when the groundhogs resumed their raids. The recently cleared fence seems to be keeping out the rabbits, all right, but with the groundhogs it is apparently up, over, and away we go, back to the purple cauliflower patch, if Chaka isn't riding line.

Until she gets back to all systems "Go," we are trying a suggestion passed along by one reader of my column, Emma Haller: setting a line of mousetraps. This may or may not discourage the animals. Would anyone like to place a bet on who will be the first to get a toe caught in a mousetrap? Already I can be classed among the walking wounded. Both eyes are swollen almost shut from gnat bites. Other bites and stings are vying for space between poison ivy blisters on arms, legs, face, and neck. A broken toe would just round out the situation nicely. Oh, well, as the saying goes, "If I didn't have bad luck I wouldn't have no luck at all."

Now is the time to go foraging for materials for future basketry, weaving, making wreath bases, and so on. What with our pond, tangled fencerows, woods, and other untamed areas, we always have a good supply of these natural materials. But anywhere along the back roads there is plenty of interesting material to be had for the picking (*after* asking, if it is on private property). You may even find stands of wheat straw, just at the right stage, which will come in handy for making Swedish stars and angels for decorations come Christmas. Just about everywhere you'll find vines, runners, roots, shoots, leaves, stems, bark, splints, grasses, sedges, reeds, and rushes.

Any kind of straw—wheat, rye, barley—should be cut by hand when in grain, tied in bundles, and stored in a dry mouse-proof place until wanted for use. Later, when you're ready to make ornaments, the straw can be dampened and kept in a plastic bag to keep it pliable. All you need is a spool of carpet thread, and you're all set to make the most charming of ornaments that will last for years and years.

Virginia creeper has tough, woody runners of a rich dark brown, effective when used alone or with other materials. Mulberry roots are a wonderful orange color; osage orange has bright yellow ones. These and other roots may be split into fine strips for weaving. The bark of cedar, maple, pine, walnut, and sassafras may also be split into strips and used in weaving; hickory, white oak, and swamp maple are also good for splints. The natural colors of all these strips are different and interesting, but if you want to use some contrasting color all of them can be dyed with natural berries like poke and elder.

July

Florida mangoes are on the market now. The price is still a bit high for buying them in quantity to make Mango Chutney for the coming winter, but not out of sight for making a fresh MANGO CHUTNEY, and nothing could be better with a curried dish or cold chicken or lamb. We like two versions of it. Both start out with a firm but fully ripe mango, peeled and cut into fairly thin slices. For No. 1, add chopped fresh mint, mustard seed, some lime juice, and coarse salt. For No. 2, add chopped fresh coriander, lemon juice, salt, and a sprinkle of chili powder. Fresh peaches are also good this way.

Back to the garden. Before long we should be getting eggplant, but while we're waiting the plants themselves are a feast for the eyes. We planted three or four different varieties, but the most handsome one is Black Nite. The stems, leaf veins, and new growth are a velvety deep purple, so dark they are almost black. By contrast the crisp deep-lavender flowers are as pretty as anything you'd see at a flower show.

Do you ever stop to look at the vegetable flowers? All of them are beautiful. The squash blossoms are big, bright gold, and handsome (no wonder they are the inspiration for the designs of the famous Indian necklaces). Bean blossoms—pink, white, lavender, and other colors—look like miniature sweet peas. Some of the vegetable flowers are so small you have to look at them through a magnifying glass to get the full effect of form and construction, but okra flowers will stop you in your tracks—big and beautiful pale-yellow circles, centered with dark brown.

With some vegetables we seldom see the flowers, since we have eaten the crop before the flowers and seed are produced. But many others that flower first put on quite a show. Stop and enjoy it now and again, while cultivating between rows or picking beans for the freezer—all you lucky people who have beans for the freezer.

A Blackberry Summer

For my taste the blackberry cone
Purpled over hedge and stone.

—Whittier

THE blackberry is probably our most valuable wild fruit. Highbush, mountain, creeping, thimbleberry—in one form or another it is found growing in old fields, along fencerows, in open woods, and in thickets. In the wild the fruit will vary considerably in size, quantity, and flavor, and in some seasons the crop will be better than others, but there always seems to be plenty of this wayside bounty to be had for the picking.

Time was when youngsters would earn spending money by picking blackberries and selling them by the gallon. This was an easy way to get plenty of this delectable fruit for juice, jelly, jam, pies, cakes, wine, cordial, or the many other good things based on the flavor and aroma of blackberry. Now it's a case of pick your own or do without. Right now it looks like being the best blackberry summer we've had in a long time. The thorny canes are laden with fruit, just beginning to turn pink, and we've had enough rain at the right time to ensure a good crop.

If you're going berrying for the first time, take along pails to hold the fruit. (It is no longer possible to find lightweight tin pails which used to be standard equipment for berry picking, but the inexpensive plastic buckets for paint mixing serve the purpose.) If you hook the bucket to your belt, you'll have both hands free to strip the berries from the vines. It's a good idea to wear something like jeans to protect your legs from scratches. You should take along an insect repellent (where there are brambles there are also chiggers and ticks), and wear a straw hat to keep your brains from getting poached in the summer sun.

Last Sunday the berry season opened for us when our

friend Mary Belle Frey came over bearing a large splint basket, heaped to the brim with fresh red raspberries. Last year she provided a Strawberry Festival on the Fourth. Having some advance notice, I planned a special meal for the event. This time she called late the night before and arrived early the next morning, so I settled for a simple sandwich-and-salad lunch, after which we *gorged* ourselves on red raspberries and cream. Each of us had a bowl heaped with berries (the old blue soup plates hold at least a pint), and the three of us polished off a pint of thick cream to top them. The sandwich wasn't bad, the salad was good, but those berries were memorable. Well, at least they were a satisfactory substitute, until the best of all brambles ripen.

Getting set for the season, I've been lining up all my favorite recipes. Just hope there will be enough berries to make them all. One of these dates from my childhood—that is, my memory of eating it goes back that far. The dish itself, called BLACKBERRY SLUMP or mush or whatever, must go back to the beginning of bread and brambles. To make it, mash ripe blackberries in a saucepan, simmer or stew in their own juice, add sugar to taste, and serve warm over a slice or two of buttered bread—with or without cream.

Blackberries make a good conventional two-crust pie but they are even better in deep-dish pies, cobblers, dumplings, or roly-poly. For BLACKBERRY ROLY-POLY, roll biscuit dough ½ inch thick, brush with melted butter, pile on 3 C blackberries, ½ C sugar, and a sprinkle of cinnamon. Fold the dough over to make a roll, place it in a buttered baking dish or pan, and around the sides put 3 C berries that have been tossed with ½ C sugar. Bake in a hot oven (375°) until crust is brown. Serve warm, sliced and topped with the berry sauce in the pan.

For BLACKBERRY COBBLER mix 3 C berries with ⅔ C sugar and place in buttered casserole or baking pan. Dot with butter and top with biscuit dough (either made into single crust or cut in small rounds and spaced close together). Bake in hot oven (375°) until topping is crisp and brown.

BLACKBERRY PUDDING may be steamed or baked and is usually served with a sweet sauce. Sprinkle 1 quart of berries with ¼ C each of flour and sugar. Toss to coat berries evenly. To 2 C bread crumbs add 4 C hot milk and a pinch of salt; then fold in the coated berries. Pour into buttered pudding dish and steam for 1 hour, or bake 45 minutes in a 350° oven.

BLACKBERRY JAM is not only delicious on hot biscuits, corn muffins, or home-baked loaf bread, it is essential to one of the best of all moist, rich cakes. (I'm talking about the real thing, made with seeds and all.) Wash and pick over blackberries and crush them slightly to release juice. To each C of berries and juice add ¾ C sugar. Cook, stirring frequently until it reaches desired consistency, and seal in sterilized jars.

I have baked my way through an extensive file of recipes for BLACKBERRY JAM CAKE, but after trying others I usually come back to one of the simplest and best, an adaptation of one found in *A Careful Compilation of Tried and Approved Recipes Gleaned by the Ladies' Aid Society of the Park Avenue Methodist Church, Rich Hill, Missouri*. To 2 C sifted cake flour add 1 tsp soda, a pinch of salt, and ½ tsp each of cloves, allspice, and cinnamon. Sift together two or three times. In electric mixer cream 1 C sugar with ⅔ C butter. When fluffy, add 2 whole eggs and 2 egg yolks and blend at slightly higher speed until mixture is smooth. Then, turning to lowest speed, add the flour and spice mixture alternately with ¼ C buttermilk and 1 C blackberry jam. Bake in greased, floured, layer-cake tins in 375° oven. Fill and ice with seven-minute frosting made with the 2 reserved egg whites.

Of course a lot of blackberry goodies require some method of divorcing the juice from the pulp and seeds. This procedure can be messy and time-consuming, but it need not be, thanks to the Saftborn. This dandy contraption is a three-section container. The fruit, vegetable, or whatever you want to dejuice goes into a perforated basket at the top, in the base there is a section for water, and in the middle is a holding station where the steamed juice collects to be drained off into sterilized bottles or jars (for future use) or made up immediately. Incidentally, the Saftborn is also excellent for steam-cooking corn, cabbage, and other vegetables. It should be just the thing for extracting the juice from beet stems and leaves for making borscht, getting the essence of various herbs to be used in flavoring vinegar, not to mention the many fruits that can be turned into juice for processing or made into jellies, syrups, cordials, and such. And no more messing about with jelly bags, letting fruit drip overnight.

Meanwhile, back to the blackberry juice. For BLACKBERRY JELLY add ¾ C sugar to each C of juice, stir until sugar is dissolved, bring to boil, and cook rapidly to jelly stage. Pour into sterilized glasses or jars, top with paraffin, and cover.

BLACKBERRY SYRUP is marvelous on waffles and pancakes or used as a sauce for puddings, ice cream, and other desserts. Combine the same proportions of juice and sugar as for jelly but don't cook it as long; then pour into sterilized bottles and seal.

Blackberry Cordial is in a class by itself. Back in Abingdon, Virginia, Miss Annie White could never understand why everyone who came to visit seemed to need her specific remedy for "the Summer Complaint"! The answer was easy (only nobody ever told her): hints of having this difficulty were the only way to get Miss Annie to break out a bottle of her Blackberry Cordial.

There are several approaches to making a delicious BLACKBERRY CORDIAL. Here is an excellent one. To 1 gallon blackberry juice add 4 pounds sugar, 4 pieces cinnamon stick, 1 tsp grated nutmeg, and about 20 whole cloves. Boil until down to ½ original volume and strain through filter paper placed over a sieve. To the filtered syrup add 1 quart good brandy. Store in sterilized bottles with screw tops. (With the Saftborn I think I can get around having to filter this by steaming the spices with the fruit while the juice is being extracted.)

Curses in the Corn Patch and Other Places

*The gay raccoon, by the light of the moon,
    was combing her auburn hair.*
                                            —*"Animal Fair"*

JUST put a radio in the corn patch, our neighbor, Tweed Howser, said; that will keep the coons out of your sweet corn. I had already proved that sprinkling black pepper and planting pumpkins around the corn didn't work, but being ever trusting, at my wits' end, and willing to try *anything*, we rigged up a radio. We put it in a large metal can to intensify the sound, tuned in to an all-night station that broadcasts everything from acid rock to hymns-that-touch-the-heart, and turned the volume to full blast. (Fortunately we don't have any *near* neighbors, either up- or downwind.)

The idea may have worked for Tweed, but over here the gay raccoon wasn't spending time combing her auburn hair. She and her cousins and her sisters and her aunts were dancing to tunes by the light of the moon and having a high old time ripping off ears, stripping back the shucks, and feasting on tender just-ready-to-eat Seneca Chief corn. Not satisfied to eat their fill and run, they obviously had plans to carry off the whole crop. I found some ears neatly piled up close to the patch, with more piled up by the fence and over on the other side. They must have had an assembly line going, with some to pick, others to fetch and carry, but something must have interrupted them in the middle of Operation Corn Caper. Probably Chaka.

Just at daylight I went out the back door and saw her standing "on point" under the maple tree. Looked up and saw she had a coon treed. First I whistled up Jim, who came out with his pistol, took aim, and shot several times. Heck, he didn't even hit the tree, much less the raccoon sitting in it.

It was early to call Butch but I went ahead and did so, telling him that if he wanted to bring down his rifle one of the Garden Raiders was a sitting target in the maple tree. He lost no time in getting down here and brought down the coon with one shot.

When the excitement was over I inspected Chaka. Raccoons are fierce animals to tangle with; not only their teeth but also those wicked slashing claws can do a lot of damage. Chaka had one deep scratch across her muzzle and some damage to an ear, both of which cleared up and healed in a day or so. An overlooked slash on her paw became infected, but after an overnight stay at the "hospital" and a few days of bedrest at home she was back on her feet and running, patrolling the fence line.

Since the fence seems to be rabbit-proof at ground line, and so far as I know rabbits can't climb fences and Chaka is catching a lot of them *outside* the fence—but we are still getting rabbit damage—I've come to the conclusion we have fenced them *in!* That underneath the entire garden is a vast rabbit warren, sort of a Watership Down West. Nothing else can account for the fact that some of the crops continue to get eaten back.

Each time the peas get about 5 inches high they get nibbled back to the ground. I give them a booster shot of nitrate of soda, they come back in a hurry, promptly get eaten—and then the cycle starts all over again. It has happened five times and it is getting to all of us in different ways. All of us includes Butch, who is doing the heavy work in the garden this season in exchange for half the harvest; Carol, his wife, who frequently comes with him to unwind dodder and pull weeds; and little Kelly, who loves to plant seed and does a good job of it.

When I go out in the morning and see what has happened, there is raving and ranting in the pea patch. Later,

Butch inspects the damage and says nothing but groans a lot. Little Kelly stamps her foot and declares, "Well, if that's the way they're going to act, I'm just not going to plant any more seed." But Carol, poor Carol. She doesn't say anything, but she *dreams*. Her dreams are of shelling peas, pod after pod, all night long, but when she opens the pods there aren't any peas—just rows of eensie-weensie rabbits.

A Surfeit of Squash

Git outen the way, Ol' Dan Tucker,
You're too late to git your supper.
Supper's done and the dishes washed,
Nothin' left but a piece of squash.
—Folk song

THE song doesn't say whether Dan Tucker finished up that "piece of squash." If the season was well along he may have decided that you *can* get too much of a good thing. Few garden vegetables produce such a bountiful and continuous crop, and once the plants hit their stride the situation begins to get out of hand. Coping with the squash crop can seem like a full-time career for the family cook. You can steam, fry, bake, stuff, boil, run through a vast repertoire of recipes—and then, by gosh, there's more squash.

Fortunately, the flavor and texture of each is different, and they all combine well with other vegetables, meats, and different seasonings. From the just-opened blossoms to those "biggies" that hide under the leaves until they are suddenly a foot long, there are interesting ways to prepare squash at every size and stage.

The crisp texture and delicate flavor of FRIED SQUASH BLOSSOMS give a pleasing contrast when served with creamy casseroles of other summer vegetables. Select male blossoms (the ones that do not have any small fruit forming at the base), cut them off close to the base as soon as they open, dip them in batter, and deep fry. (Do *not* cut blossoms from plants that have just been sprayed.)

At the earliest stage, when the baby squash are no more than 1 inch across or 2 inches long, they make a marvelous GARLIC HERB PICKLE. Green, white, and yellow types can be combined, and tiny green tomatoes, sweet peppers, cucumbers, and other vegetables may be added to them. Pack baby vegetables in sterilized pint jars and add to each one 1 clove garlic, 1 small hot pepper, and a spray of fresh dill or fennel (or ½ tsp dried seed). Cover with boiling hot brine made of 1 quart water, 2 C vinegar, and ½ C kosher salt, and seal. I make up this amount of brine, enough for several pints, and keep it in the refrigerator for use as small vegetables become available.

STEAMED SQUASH. When the squash babies get a bit larger, no more than 2 or 3 inches long, the best way to cook them is the simplest: just steam them whole and then add butter, coarse salt, and freshly ground pepper before serving.

When the yellow straight or crookneck squash get up to slicing size, I make YELLOW SQUASH SUPREME. Dice 2 slices of bacon, fry until crisp, lift from fat, and drain on a paper towel. To remaining bacon fat add 3 or 4 squash, cut into ½-inch slices. Cover and cook on medium heat until just tender. Before serving add coarse salt and a light sprinkle of chili powder and top with crisp bacon bits.

The best thing to do with yellow squash when it gets on the large side is to make SQUASH PUDDING, which is especially good served with roast chicken or ham. Cook about 4 C chopped squash in just enough water to steam. When tender, mash with a fork, add 1 tsp salt, freshly ground pepper, 1 beaten egg, ¼ C cream, and enough fine cracker crumbs to bind the mixture. Top with buttered crumbs and grated cheese and bake at 350° until lightly browned.

A Surfeit of Squash

SQUASH SOUP is another way to use the yellow ones of this size. For the soup base, cook any amount of squash, coarsely chopped, with half as much water, by measure, and chopped onion, allowing 1 onion for every 3 or 4 squash. When tender, either puree in the blender or put through the food mill. At this stage the base can be frozen for future use or made into a soup to be served hot or cold. To each cup of base add 1 C each of chicken broth and rich milk or cream. Season to taste with coarse salt, freshly ground pepper, and celery salt. Serve topped with a dab of sour cream, some chopped fresh dill or chives, and a dash of paprika. To prepare hot soup from frozen base use the same proportions of liquids, adding chicken broth to base, cover, and cook over low heat until base is thawed and blended with broth. Just before serving add milk or cream, season to taste, and reheat. (The same type of cream soup base can be made of almost any fresh vegetables, using the same proportions suggested for squash; this is a good way to utilize the tougher ends of asparagus. Green or yellow wax beans, peas, lettuce, broccoli, and cauliflower or corn are all good, too.)

Cymlins or pattypans (or whatever you happen to call the white scalloped squash—our youngsters called them "petticoat squash") have the most delicate flavor of all types of summer squash. As long as they are tender enough for the skin to be easily pierced by thumbnail, they can be prepared in a number of ways. When they are too large to steam whole, try STEWED CYMLINS. Cut young squash into slices or chunks, add just enough water to keep them from burning, cover, and cook over medium heat until tender. Mash lightly with a fork, turn into a serving dish, and season with butter, salt, and freshly ground pepper.

For DEEP-FRIED CYMLINS slice squash into bite-size pieces, dip them in flour and then into beaten egg, and coat with fine bread crumbs. Let chill for at least 1 hour and then fry in deep fat until golden brown. Drain on a paper towel and serve with any simple tomato sauce.

When the cymlins are under 4 inches in size they make attractive individual servings of STUFFED CYMLINS. Allow 1 squash for each serving. Scoop out center, from stem end, and set aside, leaving a shell about ½ inch thick. Blanch shells in boiling water for 1 minute or so, lift out with slotted spoon, and place upside down on towels to drain. To each cup of reserved pulp of cymlin add 1 T each chopped scallions and green peppers and about ½ C fresh corn pulp. Stir and cook in 1 T butter for about 5 minutes. Add about ½ C heavy sweet or sour cream and enough bread crumbs to bind the mixture. Season to taste with salt, pepper, and fresh thyme or marjoram. Heap the mixture into the drained shells and top with buttered crumbs and wheat germ. Place in a buttered shallow pan, cover lightly with foil, and bake about 30 minutes at 350°; then remove cover and continue baking until top is lightly browned.

When the cymlin skins reach the stage where they have to be peeled—which happens rather rapidly—I forget about cooking them and use them for decoration. A few of them heaped in a wooden bowl or a basket, with some fresh green foliage, looks cool and pretty. Sometimes I add them to arrangements of other vegetables and flowers, and when they get on the big side I scoop them out to leave a shell, fill the centers with damp oasis, and use them as interesting containers for arrangements of summer flowers and grasses.

Zucchinis, cocozelles, French courgettes: these are the green summer squashes that have a very firm texture and more pronounced flavor than the white and yellow types. I call them all zukes and use them interchangeably. They can all be substituted for cucumbers in most pickle and relish recipes. Any size up to about 6 inches is good to slice or cut into sticks and chill in crushed ice, to be dipped into coarse salt and eaten—instead of salad—with dishes like Italian spaghetti. Or these raw slices or sticks may be added to any mixed green salad.

At the same size, ZUKE SAUTÉ makes a good dish for luncheon or a summer supper. For each serving cook 2 strips of lean bacon until crisp, drain on a paper towel, and pour off most of the fat. To the remaining fat in the skillet, add zukes cut into ¼-inch slices, allowing at least 1 C of slices for each serving. As slices are lightly browned on one side, turn and cook on other side. Cover and steam for a minute or two, remove from heat, sprinkle with salt and pepper, turn out on platter, and serve with crisp bacon strips.

There is hardly any way you can combine zukes with tomatoes, onions, peppers, eggplants, olive oil, fennel, basil, or oregano and not come up with something good. They all just naturally go together. Combinations of this type are generally found under the general heading of RATATOUILLE. My variations on the theme depend on how much of what I can find in the garden. Proportions do not have to be exact, but here is a good basic recipe to build on. If you like garlic, start by cooking 1 minced clove of garlic in 2 T olive oil and add 1 medium-size unpeeled eggplant, cut into ½-inch slices. Brown lightly, turn, and top with a layer of sliced zukes, 1 large onion cut in ¼-inch slices, 1 or 2 sweet green or red peppers seeded and cut into strips, and 3 or 4 large fresh tomatoes, peeled and cut into thick slices. Season with coarse salt, freshly ground pepper, 1 T molasses, and some stems of fresh basil, oregano, and parsley. Cover and cook over medium heat until vegetables are tender, or cook in a shallow casserole in a moderate oven.

Throughout the garden season I make this at least two or three times a week, each time doing enough to serve one meal with extra amounts to go in the freezer, packed in pint and quart containers. Even if I had to buy the makings at a roadside market I would do the same, for it is so good and so endlessly useful. It may be served alone, hot or cold, with nothing more than some crusty bread, fresh from the oven. It is delicious with any type of roast or broiled meat; it also makes a fine sauce for omelets, broiled or fried fish, and any type of pasta, usually topped with freshly grated Parmesan or Romano cheese.

SUMMER CASSEROLE is different in flavor and

makes a marvelous main dish that can be cooked ahead, kept warm, and then carried out to the terrace or to a picnic to be served when everybody gets hungry. I make it in a shallow oval casserole—the 11-inch size will serve 6, the next larger one makes enough for about 10 portions. In the bottom of the casserole start with a layer of zukes, cut into ½-inch slices, and over it place layers of the following vegetables: fresh corn scraped from ears, fresh lima beans, sliced okra, onions, green peppers, and tomatoes. Sprinkle with salt, freshly ground pepper, and minced parsley. Make the top layer of closely spaced patties of fresh pork sausage that has been seasoned with sage. Cover casserole lightly with foil and bake about 45 minutes at 350°. Remove foil and continue baking until the sausage is lightly browned. Serve with French bread to sop up every drop of that marvelous juice of mingled meat and vegetable flavors, have a jug of wine on the side and some fresh fruit to finish up with, and there you have a fine meal, put together with a minimum of fuss.

ZUKE CUSTARD can't be kept on "hold" or transported any distance, but it makes a good main event for a light summer luncheon. Coarsely shred enough zukes to measure about 3 C and put in bottom of well-buttered baking dish—about a 7-inch size. Cover with combination of 2 eggs well beaten with 1 C rich milk or cream and seasoned to taste, with 1 C grated sharp cheese added. Bake at 350° until custard is set and lightly browned on top. Serve immediately. This is very good with fried tomatoes and bacon, or sliced cold roast, or chicken and fresh tomatoes.

There are so many things with which you can stuff zukes that almost anything goes, but about the most elegant is MASAKO'S STUFFED ZUKE. (Masako Herron is a very talented designer, and everything she does reflects a feeling for color and form—even the way she arranges food on a plate.) Cut a top slice from a fairly large zuke, scrape all pulp from this lid, and remove enough seeds and pulp from the case to make a "shell" about ½ inch thick. Blanch this shell in boiling water for 2 or 3 minutes, lift out with tongs, hold under running cold water until chilled, and then drain, upside down, over paper towels. While it is draining, prepare stuffing. Make a fairly thick cream sauce, using 3 T each butter and flour and 1 C cream. Season to taste with salt, lemon juice, and Tabasco. Gently fold in 1 pound of backfin lump crab and mound into zuke shell. Sprinkle top with grated Parmesan and bake at 350° until top is lightly browned. If you have more of the crab-and-sauce mix than needed to fill the shell, bake it in a custard cup.

When the "biggies" have gone beyond the size to use for anything else, they will still make a delicious moist bread. For ZUKE-BRAN BREAD—enough for two medium-size loaves—in an electric mixer bowl combine 4 eggs, 1 C firmly packed dark brown sugar, and 1 C vegetable oil and mix at high speed until well blended. Add 1 C All-Bran to soak in liquid. Sift together 3½ C flour, 1½ tsp each of salt and soda, ¾ tsp baking powder, 1 tsp ground cinnamon, and ¼ tsp each ground allspice and nutmeg. Wash and shred 3 C zuke. Slowly blend dry ingredients and shredded zuke into liquids with 1 tsp vanilla. Fold in 1 C chopped pecans or ½ C each pecans and chopped dates. Turn into greased pans and bake at 350° about 1 hour.

FREEZING SQUASH. Both the yellow and green squashes freeze well, if you handle them correctly. When they are no more than 1½ inches across, wash and dry them, cut into ½-inch slices, and immediately space in single layers on cookie sheets and pop into freezer. As soon as they are partially frozen, shift the slices to plastic bags, seal, and return to freezer. When you're ready to cook them, all you have to do is remove as many slices as you need for a meal.

When the squashes get larger I cut them into cubes and add them to other mixed vegetables I'm freezing for soups and stews. (When I bring in vegetables, fresh from the garden, to prepare and freeze at once in small amounts, I never blanch them. What blanching does is stop enzyme action, but the quick freezing serves the same purpose.)

AUGUST
Barricades, Beetles, Broodies, and Lazy Beans

*Rain, rain, go away,
And come again another day.*
—Nursery rhyme

I'M beginning to feel like the preacher who prayed for rain. Soon after it came on to rain, and it rained, and it rained, and it rained. After two weeks with no letup, he offered up another prayer. "Dear Lord, we thank thee, but this is *ridiculous*."

Saint Swithin's Day was the fifteenth. If it rained that day—and it did—we're supposed to be in for forty more days of the same. If this is the case, we'll all be afloat. Already there is a lot of fungus among us—mold, mildew, and mushrooms galore. I have seen ten different mushroom species out under the oak tree by the stable. All are pretty, *some* are edible. Many of the wild mushrooms have a distinctive and delicious flavor, but they're nothing to mess around with unless you *know* what you're doing. Much better to pass up this pleasure than to take chances on going on to Old Stony Lonesome ahead of schedule.

Seldom do I find time to sit in the garden, but I keep

Barricades, Beetles, Broodies, and Lazy Beans

a folding stool out there, for the occasions when my knees begin to buckle or I need to take a breather and fan my brow. But the other evening I sat down to contemplate and cogitate. No, the better-mousetrap idea didn't work. Yes, they're at it again! Rabbits found a new way under the fence and had a picnic in the soybean patch. Doubtless having had his fill of tomatoes and cauliflower, the groundhog went on to pull down the 3-foot vines of Sweet Slice cucumbers and eat them back to nubbins.

While sitting there, pondering what to do next (my ingenuity and patience about run out), I was diverted by a hummingbird that came within a foot or so of where I was sitting, to sip nectar from the lavender blooms on the eggplant. After darting in and out and around these plants, it made a short detour for nectar dessert at the Pink Champagne lily. A pretty sight, but this was no time for bird-watching.

Back to the cucumbers, I put up an additional fence barricade around what remained of the vines. Later, I wondered if the groundhog had a good laugh, watching me, for while I was in the house for a short time, he returned to the scene of the crime and went on to sample vines of Jet and Parisian Pickling cucumbers thriving nearby.

This really tied the rag on the bush, adding insult to injury. It took several hours but finally I managed to catch him in the act and, armed with a hoe, got him cornered. For a while there it was Mexican Standoff, but eventually Chaka arrived on the scene, I got the gate opened, she slipped through, and with one clamp of those jaws that particular groundhog had had his last cucumber.

As everyone must know by now, the Jap beetles are back with a vengeance. Since DDT is a no-no, about the best spray to use is Sevin. Ordinarily, it can be applied about every seven days, but in weather like this it should be used after every rain. The liquid Sevin costs a bit more than the wettable dust, but with it there is no mixing, straining, or getting a clogged sprayer. (Is there anything more conducive to a coronary arrest than having a pressure tank full of spray that won't come out the nozzle? Especially on a hot, muggy day.) Another blessing is the trombone sprayer. With this gadget, a plastic bucket, and a liquid spray I can mix and apply garden spray without assistance, sweat, curses, or tears, and that's more than can be said for any other system.

Tom Taylor reports a different problem: his pole beans won't climb. His beans are either lazy or tired, but in any case they tend to sprawl. He thinks this is just a part of the present breakdown in the natural order of things, other evidences being that his laying hens won't go broody, pants are no longer made with watch pockets, and some of the pepper plants I gave him "shrink" instead of growing. I couldn't help him with the watch-pocket problem (could have suggested that he wear a shoulder purse to hold his watch, but doubt if the idea would have grabbed him), but I diagnosed the pepper plant problem as being due to the shock of moving them from this "thin" soil at the eastern end of the county into that Loudoun Valley loam at "Coolbrook." After all, the first meal after a long fast shouldn't be a banquet.

About the hens, they're scatter-brain critters at best. When eggs are a glut on the market, they lay eggs. When eggs get scarce they stop laying and start to molt, doing nothing more productive than messily dropping feathers all over the place. If you want them to settle down and go broody, they spend their time racing around squawking and shrieking and flapping their wings, pretending they're trying to elude lusty young roosters.

If you want them to go broody before they're of a mind to, it usually works to let their eggs pile up in the nest instead of collecting them daily. (Or you can slip out the freshly laid eggs and replace them with "nest eggs.") If you want to "break up" a hen who is determined to start setting, either put her in a "broody coop," which is raised above the floor and has a wire bottom, or keep her nest filled with ice cubes. Either of these methods will cool off any inclinations she has to stay on the nest for the next three weeks.

As for the beans, in my experience climbing beans are like children. Sometimes you have to gently, or even sometimes firmly, train them in the way they should go.

Pickle Time

*Peter Piper picked a peck of pickle peppers,
A peck of pickle peppers Peter Piper picked.*
—Tongue-twister

SIGNS of the season: tomatoes hanging heavy on the vine, ripe peaches at every roadside stand, peppers by the peck and everything else by the bushel. All are reminders that it is high time to start those good spicy smells coming from the kitchen, if you want a well-stocked pickle and relish shelf this coming winter. Don't wait until the garden vegetables get too big or seasonal fruits are past their prime. The end result in the pickle jar will be no better than the ingredients you start with. Fruits should be firm, vegetables should be on the young side.

Before you start, check your equipment and supplies. Don't wait until the last minute and then have to make a mad dash from place to place, trying to locate some elusive ingredient that has suddenly and mysteriously disappeared from the shelves. For all canning and pickling you should use kosher salt. Vinegar—either cider or white distilled—should be fresh, 5-percent strength. Just look on the label for the acidity percentage. The containers in which you soak vegetables in brine or other solutions should be ceramic or glass; even a square plastic dishpan will do. Just don't use certain metal containers that may affect flavor and color. For the same reason, use only cooking kettles that are enamel-coated or stainless steel.

Be sure all your knives are sharp, and here's a hint on how to get them that way and keep them that way. Over the years I have gained and lost a succession of paring knives. Probably because I keep them razor sharp and always take them along to flower shows and demonstrations for special cutting jobs, invariably someone borrows my knife of the moment and "forgets" to return it. On the other hand, however, my prize slicing knife has been in use longer than I have (and right now that seems like a long, long time). Doubtless it was purchased by someone, somewhere, sometime. I happened to inherit it, and since it has been in my possession almost forty years it has been kept razor sharp by constant whetting on the edge of an old crock or mixing bowl with unglazed rim.

Every kitchen ought to have at least one of these old crocks or bowls, and every cook should know how to sharpen knives on them. It is a handy, easy way to keep a knife in trim and never get a dull edge. Several times during any cutting, chopping, or slicing job I give the knife a swipe or two over the crock edge. It has become such a habit it is just part of the rhythm of anything I happen to be doing with the knife. I'm sure that if I had to stop what I was doing and get out a whetstone or steel, or otherwise make a production of restoring the sharp edge to a knife, my cutting equipment would be as dull as that found in most kitchens.

But enough about knives. Let us press on with the pickles. When cucumbers get to be about 1¼ inches across they are just right for SUPER SWEET PICKLE CHIPS, which are the easiest sweet type to make. The super thing about them is the crisp texture. Wash about 7 pounds of cucumbers and, using a ripple cutter if possible, cut into ¼-inch slices. Add slices to 1 gallon of cold water mixed with 2 C slaked or hydrated lime (found at garden centers and farm supply stores) and let soak overnight. Next morning drain cucumbers, cover with fresh water and some crushed ice, and let stand for 3 hours. Drain again, place in large preserving kettle, and cover with boiling-hot solution made of 2 quarts cider vinegar, 4½ pounds granulated sugar, 1 T kosher salt, and 1 tsp each celery seed, whole cloves, and mixed pickling spices. Let stand 35 minutes. Move kettle to stove, heat until boiling, and then pack into hot sterilized jars and seal immediately.

Over the years I've tried numerous variations of chutney, using different combinations of fruits and spices. All have been good, but MANGO-PEACH CHUTNEY is choice. In a large enamel preserving kettle combine 3 C each brown sugar and cider vinegar and the thinly slivered rind and juice of 3 lemons. Simmer and stir until sugar is dissolved. Add 1 T kosher salt, 2 T whole mustard seed, 2 cloves minced garlic, 1 seeded hot pepper cut into thin slivers, ½ C candied ginger cut into thin strips, 2 large onions cut into ¼-inch slices and then cut across to make cubes of the same size, 2 T shredded fresh ginger root, ½ tsp each freshly ground nutmeg, black pepper, and cardamon, ¼ tsp ground cloves, 1 tsp ground ginger, 2 tsp cumin, and 1 T each turmeric and coriander. Simmer syrup about 5 minutes. Add 2 large sweet peppers, seeded and cut in ¼-inch strips, 3 mangoes cut in ¼-inch slices, 1 C seedless raisins or ½ C each raisins and currants. Then peel, pit, slice, and add enough firm ripe peaches to bring fruit to top of syrup. Bring mixture to boil and cook fairly rapidly, stirring frequently to prevent scorching, until syrup is thickened. Do *not* overcook, and be careful not to crush fruits when stirring. Ladle into hot sterilized jars and seal immediately.

I've never bothered to experiment with WATERMELON PICKLE recipes because the one I have always used makes the best ever. It does take three days to make but is worth it. On day one, peel and remove all pink flesh from watermelon rind. Using ripple cutter, cut into pieces about 1 by 1½ inches in size. To about 8 pounds of this prepared rind, add ½ C slaked lime and 1 gallon of cold water. Let soak overnight. On day two, drain rind, sprinkle with ⅓ C alum, cover with boiling water, and let stand 5 minutes. Drain rind in colander and hold under cold running water until it is chilled. Cover rind with clear water and boil for 30 minutes. Drain again. To enough water to cover rind, add 1 box of dried ginger root, boil for 30 minutes to make a strong ginger tea, add rind, and boil in ginger tea for 30 minutes. Drain rind and add to hot syrup made of 8 pounds granulated sugar, 6 C cider vinegar, and 1 T each whole cloves, allspice, and stick cinnamon. Cover container, set aside, and let stand until next day. On day three, bring syrup-covered rind to boil, uncovered, and simmer until chunks are translucent. Ladle pickle chunks into hot sterilized jars, cover with the boiling syrup, and seal. This makes a pickle that is crisp as an icicle, yet tender. When we come to the end of the pickles in a jar I save the syrup to use for glazing baked ham. Later, the juice from the ham and glaze is used to flavor various vegetable combinations. I added some to a batch of Ratatouille the other day and the flavor was *great*.

There are two types of tomato relish we like and use a lot. They are very different in flavor but both are equally good. RED RELISH calls for 1 peck of very firm, just-ripe tomatoes, 3 large onions, 4 large sweet red peppers, 1 large green pepper, 2 fresh hot peppers (all seeded), and 3 C coarsely chopped celery. Using large blade in food grinder, grind all vegetables. Sprinkle with ½ C kosher salt and let stand overnight. Drain in colander on following morning. In preserving kettle, combine 6 C each granulated sugar and cider vinegar, 4 T mustard seed, 3 T celery seed, and 1 T powdered cinnamon. Bring to hard boil. Add drained vegetables, bring to boil again, and cook for 5 minutes. Ladle into hot sterilized jars and seal.

For GREEN RELISH, chop ¾ peck green tomatoes, 1 quart onions, and 6 large sweet peppers (3 green and 3 red). Sprinkle with ½ C kosher salt, cover with crushed ice, and let stand overnight. Next morning drain thoroughly in colander. Put drained vegetables in preserving kettle with 1 box mustard seed and 6 C each dark brown sugar and cider vinegar. Add 1 quart jar of dill pickles that have been drained and chopped. (Be sure to use regular dill pickles and *not* the kosher type, which have a different texture and a strong garlic flavor.) Bring relish mixture to boil and cook about 5 minutes. Ladle into hot sterilized jars and seal.

A four-generation favorite in the family is HIGDON

SALAD, a mixed vegetable relish that is always served with baked beans, added to chopped meats for sandwich spreads, and used in dozens of other ways. Chop, medium fine, 4 quarts cabbage, 1 quart onions, 2 quarts each green tomatoes and cucumbers (or zucchini), 6 large sweet peppers (3 red, 3 green), and 2 hot red peppers. Mix all together, sprinkle with ½ C kosher salt, and let stand several hours or overnight. Drain vegetables thoroughly. Dump into preserving kettle, add 6 C each brown sugar and cider vinegar, 4 T mustard seed, 2 T celery seed, and 1 T each powdered ginger, turmeric, cinnamon, and cloves. Bring to boil, cook about 5 minutes, ladle into sterilized jars, and seal.

DOROTHY'S ONION RELISH does not include any of the usual pickling spices, so it is different *and* delicious. Peel and very thinly slice 14 medium-size onions; add 6 large sweet peppers, seeded and finely chopped, and 2 seeded hot peppers cut into thin slivers. Cover with boiling water, let stand 4 minutes, and drain. Cover with boiling water again and let stand 4 minutes; then drain. In preserving kettle combine 4 C white distilled vinegar, 3 C granulated sugar, and 2 T kosher salt. Bring to boil. Add onion mixture, cook on medium heat 15 minutes, ladle into hot sterilized jars, and seal.

Had a request from a reader on a sugar-free diet who had a craving for some kind of sweet pickles, and a big crop of cukes coming from the garden. He couldn't find any recipes calling for sugar substitutes and before starting to experiment wanted to know what sugar does besides making things sweet. Depending on the amount used, sugar does two things: acts as a preservative and affects flavor. In using sugar substitutes we have to allow for the fact that they do not act as a preservative and with them we do not get the same consistency. For instance, it is possible to make quite good preserves or jams with sugar substitutes, but some thickening agent must be added, only small quantities should be made at one time, and they must be stored in the refrigerator.

Any pickle recipe that calls for sufficient vinegar to act as a preservative could possibly be adapted to use a sugar-free sweetener, but here is an old tried-and-true one for SACCHARINE PICKLES. Wash and pack 2 quarts small to medium-size whole cucumbers in sterilized jars; add 1 tsp mixed pickling spices to each jar and cover cukes with a boiling liquid made of ¼ tsp saccharine, ¼ C each of kosher salt and dry mustard, and 1 quart vinegar; and seal.

For SUGAR-FREE BREAD AND BUTTER PICKLES, cut into fairly thin slices 7 medium-size cucumbers and 2 large onions and add 1 large sweet pepper that has been seeded and cut into thin strips. Sprinkle with 2 T kosher salt, let stand 3 hours, and drain. In a preserving kettle combine 1¼ C cider vinegar, 1 tsp each mustard seed and celery seed, ¼ tsp turmeric, and 4 whole cloves and sweeten to taste with liquid sugar-free sweetener. Bring to boil, add drained vegetables, bring to boil again, ladle immediately into sterilized jars, and seal.

Regular BREAD AND BUTTER PICKLES are made by this same recipe, adding 1¼ C brown sugar instead of a substitute. Flavor can be varied by using white vinegar and granulated sugar, and zucchinis can be used instead of cucumbers.

The Tyranny of Tomatoes

If you can't take the heat, get out of the kitchen.
           —*H. S. Truman (among others)*

But what, I wonder, if you can't take the heat but likewise can't keep out of the kitchen?

One night last week I experienced what might be called a "tomato sauna." From right after dinner until later than I care to remember I was standing over a hot stove, stirring chili sauce. The coolest part of the kitchen must have been around 110°. I hesitate to think what the temperature was over in my particular hot spot, where the ambient air was heavy with vinegar fumes and tomato steam. I just know it was too darned hot, as the song says, and I began to wonder if there isn't something to be said for *not* having a garden. Then I thought of all the good things we would miss if we didn't have that tomato patch and decided "mustn't grumble."

But, getting back to that CHILI SAUCE: Peel, core, and cut in large chunks 1 gallon of ripe tomatoes. Add 2 C chopped onion, 4 chopped sweet peppers, and 1 medium-size hot pepper. Put prepared vegetables in preserving kettle, add 1½ C brown sugar, 2 C cider vinegar, 5 tsp kosher salt, 2 tsp ground ginger, 1 tsp each dry mustard, cinnamon, and grated nutmeg, and 1½ tsp curry powder. Bring to boil and cook until thick, stirring frequently. When it has reached desired consistency, pour into sterilized jars or bottles and seal. (This can be made at any season by substituting an institution-size (6-pound 6-ounce) can of whole tomatoes for the fresh ones.)

In addition to using this sauce as is—and I must say Jim eats it with a spoon if there isn't anything handy to put it on—a spoonful or two of it peps up gravies, sauces, soups, and stews. I usually put up about 45 pints of it to see us through to the next season.

In one form or another we eat a lot of tomatoes, year-round, and never seem to tire of them. I put up at least 50 quarts of whole tomatoes in herb-flavored juice and another 40 quarts of the juice alone, and a lot of things that include tomatoes go into the freezer: spaghetti sauce, ratatouille, chili con carne, and so on. And when they are coming in, fresh from the garden, we can, and frequently do, have tomatoes three times a day and in between.

For a hearty breakfast, nothing is better than FRIED TOMATOES. Allow 2 strips of bacon and 1 green or red tomato for each serving. Cook bacon until crisp and drain on a paper towel. Trim tomato ends, cut in ½-inch slices, dip in flour or cornmeal, and quickly fry in bacon fat until brown on both sides. Season with coarse salt and freshly ground pepper.

If you have hot biscuits to go with them, all the better, and TOMATO GRAVY rounds everything out. Pour excess fat from skillet, leaving about 2 T grease and all the crusty bits in pan. Add 2 T flour, stir until lightly browned, then add 2 C rich milk and cook, stirring constantly, until gravy is thickened. Season to taste with salt and pepper.

Of course fried tomatoes don't have to be restricted to breakfast; they're also mighty good for luncheon or supper, especially when served with something like scalloped potatoes and ham or a macaroni-and-cheese casserole. They also freeze well. After they are fried I slip the slices onto flat foil trays and pop them right into the freezer. As soon as they are firm I stack the trays, enclose them in a large plastic bag, seal, and return to freezer. When I want to serve them I just take out as many trays as needed, put them right in a 375° oven, and leave them until they're good and hot.

As a switch from the usual tomato sandwich, here are a couple of hot versions that always make a hit. BROILED TOMATO SANDWICH starts with a buttered slice of rye bread. Top with a slice of Lebanon bologna and add a dab of good mustard, a thick slice of ripe tomato, and a thin slice of onion. Sprinkle with salt and pepper and top with a small chunk of cheese. Heat under broiler until it is hot and bubbly. The edge of the bologna slice turns up and forms a sort of cup that holds all the juices. Different and *good*.

For GRILLED TOMATO SANDWICH spread a slice of white, oatmeal, or whole wheat bread thickly with sour cream that has been mixed with some grated cheese, add slices of tomato with salt, pepper, and some minced fresh herbs, cover with a buttered slice of bread, and cook on sandwich grill or lightly buttered frypan until light brown on both sides.

A STUFFED TOMATO makes a good light meal, and the stuffing can be just about anything you have on hand. After peeling and removing some pulp from large, fully ripe tomatoes, fill them with cottage cheese mixed with fresh herbs; or with a mixture of chopped cucumber, celery, and onion with mayonnaise; or, if you want to get fancy, with shrimp, crab, or chicken salad.

There are numerous versions of GAZPACHO, to be served either as a soup or a side dish to replace a more conventional salad. Here is the version we have frequently; served with thick slices of hot French bread, it makes a light meal. In individual bowls put some thin slices of onion, thick slices of tomato, and medium slices of cucumber. Add 1 T olive oil, ½ T red or sherry wine vinegar, a few celery seeds, and some chopped fresh coriander leaves. Stir around, and chill in refrigerator for about ½ hour before serving. Sometimes I add a few Greek olives (who says Greek and Spanish can't get together in a good cause?), and sometimes thin strips of fresh pepper go in as well. If you want to make a large bowl of it, just increase the amounts of everything. Then, at serving time, ladle it into individual bowls to be eaten with gusto, and a spoon.

I make a lot of casseroles, combining tomatoes with eggplant, zucchini, green pepper, and onions—with or without ground beef or lamb or ham—and topped with some kind of cheese. Any or all of these combinations are good and can be cooked in any quantity. They can be partially cooked in the morning for reheating at serving time, or completely cooked ahead and served cold, or frozen for later use. Nearly everyone who cooks has some version of these combinations.

Less usual is TOMATO-MACARONI CASSEROLE, which can also be assembled in the morning and heated at the last minute. Cook large-size elbow macaroni until al dente, amount determined by size of baking dish you plan to use. Drain, spray with cold water, and drain again. In well-buttered shallow baking dish, place a layer of macaroni, top with thick slices of fresh peeled tomato, sprinkle with salt, pepper, and chopped fresh basil, and cover with a layer of sour cream. Repeat these layers until dish is filled. Over the top layer of cream sprinkle some grated cheese and paprika. Bake in moderate oven until top is bubbly and golden brown.

Eventually (usually when the heat and humidity get up to the high miserables), the time comes when tomato is tyrant. No matter what I have planned to do or would like to be doing, something has to be done about those baskets of tomatoes on the shady porch, and more of them hanging ripe on the vines. Come hell or high water they have to be gotten into jars, in some form or other, and lined up on the shelves in the Futility Room.

Whenever I start—which may be any hour of the day or night—the first job is to make the herb-flavored juice. For this, the Saftborn is worth its weight in gold, for all I have to do is put water in the base, tomatoes and herbs in the steam basket, and wait a while until the hot juice is ready to be drawn off, directly into jars—having lost no flavor or aroma, and very few vitamins, along the way.

If you have to rely on a cooking kettle for making HERB-FLAVORED TOMATO JUICE, for every gallon of tomatoes (I prefer the smaller Vccroma or Cherry types, or one of the smallish old standards like Rutgers) allow ½ gallon of water, a good handful each of fresh basil, Italian parsley, and marjoram, 1 tsp celery seed, and a few green onions, including tops. Cook covered until tomatoes are very soft, then put through food mill. Set aside in cool place if it is to be used to cover jars of whole tomatoes; otherwise process immediately.

One day this week I put up 25 quarts of tomatoes and 3 extra quarts of juice. The day started *early* and I was pooped out by the end of the ordeal, but many times I have been just as tired but not accomplished as much. Over the years I've worked out a routine that saves motion and energy, with no time wasted between stages of preparation.

CANNING TOMATOES. Setting a pot of water to boil, I sort and wash tomatoes and dip them into a wire basket, a few at a time, in boiling water to blanch. As soon as the skins crack, I dump the tomatoes into the sink and continue blanching until I have enough to fill 5 quart jars (the capacity of my pressure canner). Peel, core, and drop tomatoes into clean, hot jars. Small tomatoes are used whole, others cut into half or quarter sections if necessary. Fill jars to 1 inch from top, getting a firm pack but not squashing the tomatoes. Add 1 rounded tsp kosher salt and cover with prepared juice. Insert knife around sides of jar to release all bubbles. Wipe jar rim with damp paper towel, place on lid that has been soaking in boiling water, and screw rim on firmly. As soon as 5 jars are ready, I process them in the pressure canner, either 10 minutes at 5 pounds pressure or 5 minutes at 10 pounds pressure. Remove canner from heat. When gauge registers zero open steam valve, remove canner lid, lift out hot jars (using a folded towel or tongs), and place jars in a draft-free place to cool. In the time it takes the jars to process and be ready for removal from the canner I usually have the next batch of 5 quarts ready to go.

If you have never used a pressure canner, don't be intimidated by it but *do* read and follow directions to the letter; keep your eye on the gauge and adjust heat if necessary to keep the pressure where it should be; and *don't open steam valve until gauge registers zero.*

One problem that is reported by a lot of first-time canners is jar lids that do not seal. On questioning I usually find that people have made the mistake of tightening the rims *after* the jars have been taken from canner. This is a definite no-no. Let jars of processed fruits or vegetables stand overnight before removing the rims. At this time check to be sure each lid is sealed. To test for seal, tap lid with a metal spoon; it should make a sort of *ping* sound. Feel lid top or even look at it closely, for if it is sealed it will be slightly concave. I do not recommend reprocessing and resealing unsealed jars but think it is better to use the contents right away or cook down to make a sauce or puree for freezing.

A lot of people ask about FREEZING TOMATOES. This can be done successfully if they are cooked by any method. In addition to freezing meal-size portions of any dish, tomato puree and paste can be frozen in ice cube trays, flipped out, and stored in plastic bags. There is only one way I know of that fresh tomatoes can be frozen with good results—for TOMATO SHERBET. Seal whole, peeled tomatoes and some fresh herbs in plastic bags and freeze immediately. Shortly before serving, dump frozen tomatoes and herbs in a blender or food processor and blend long enough to turn them into a sort of frappé.

SEPTEMBER
Autumn Woods

*I love to wander through the woodlands
In the soft light of an autumnal day.*
—Sarah Whitman, "A Still Day in Autumn"

I can't imagine living in a climate with no definite changes in season. Nor can I agree with William Cullen Bryant, who wrote, "The melancholy days are come, the saddest in the year." Perhaps if he had spent the summer trying to keep the grass cut and fighting an unending and unequal battle with weeds he would have welcomed the fall of the year with open arms.

Me, I can hardly wait for the first killing frost. I'm tired of feeling guilty about having the most magnificent giant ragweed, the handsomest poke. Of the bounty of summer—

including the canning, freezing, pickling, and jamming of same—I begin to feel a weariness. Then I note the prices on fresh produce at the supermarket and think, Well, perhaps I can hang in there for another month or so. There's something to be said for being able to dash out to the garden at the last minute and snatch a fresh pepper, a tomato, a cucumber, and something green for salad.

One of the most pleasant things about autumn is that it is about the best time of the year for a walk through the woods—for me, at least. Last week I just ignored everything that had to be done here and took to the woods for a few hours. It was a lovely misty, moisty morning, the air was soft, and everything was quiet and restful. The place I went is one of my favorite haunts—within a short distance, that is. Had I been able to take off for a day or so, I would have headed for Dolly Sods or the cranberry bog up near Marlinton. But even a short time spent walking through the damp woods, looking for ferns and mosses, enjoying the lovely colors of lichen-covered rocks and logs, was enough to wind down tension and refresh the spirit.

Too, the fern spores and bits of moss I brought back will furnish diversion and interest in the months to come. Anyone who has only looked at moss from a distance and thinks of it as a chunk of greenery should examine it closely, through a hand lens. Some of it looks like a forest in miniature; some types look like ferns. In fact, in the mosses and lichens we find repeated almost every form there is in nature, and the colors are every shade of green, sparkling like jewels in the misty air. Mosses and lichens can be dried and stored for *years* and then, like magic, be revived to look fresh as new when dampened with water.

The ferns are equally fascinating in a different way. Most ferns are reproduced from tiny spores, fine as dust, that develop in spore cases usually found on the underside of fertile fern fronds. These spore cases look like small dots or clusters arranged in interesting and characteristic patterns on the different fern species. Now is the right time to collect fertile fronds of several of the ferns found in this area, including maidenhair, ebony spleenwort, maidenhair spleenwort, and Christmas, lady, male, and Virginia chain ferns. A few others can be collected as late as October. The fertile fronds should be cut and placed in a paper envelope. Later, the dried leaves and chaff can be removed and the remaining spores can be planted. They are fascinating to watch at every stage of development. Anyone interested in ferns should have the Handbook No. 59 on Ferns published by the Brooklyn Botanic Garden (1000 Washington Avenue, Brooklyn, New York 11225). It costs very little and is jammed with useful information, including a good, simple method for growing spores.

While I got sidetracked on ferns and mosses, things were piling up otherwise: soybeans to be shelled and frozen, tomatoes requiring attention, a gift of crab apples to be juiced and jelled. So, having nothing else to do I went out and got damson plums.

Damsons are the devil to pit, and there is just no easy way to get around the job. But they make the best DAMSON CONSERVE. To 6 C pitted damsons add 6 C granulated sugar and the finely shredded rind and juice of 1 large orange and 2 lemons. Cook, stirring frequently, over medium heat until thick. Add about 2 C black-walnut meats, ladle into sterilized jars, and seal.

For some types of preserving I prefer to use the old-fashioned zinc lids with jar rubbers or the clamp-on glass lids with rubbers. I found the old jars when we cleared out the shed. Would you believe I found a cache of lids when I started clearing out the Futility Room this past week? Then what to my wondering eyes appeared on the shelf of Mr. Giant but the rubber rings to go with them! This may be coincidence, but I like to think of it as virtue rewarded.

This week's big project was making SAUSAGE, and it wasn't all that big a job at that, since I have an electric grinder and I didn't mess with the casing-stuffing bit this time. Starting with lean fresh pork shoulders, chill until meat is firm and easy to cut. Remove rind, cut meat from bone in slices, and cut again into strips, which go through the grinder easier than chunks do. (Before adding any seasoning I bag up a few portions of the plain ground pork to use for egg rolls and another soy-flavored dish we like.) To season I add for each pound of meat about 2 tsp kosher salt, ½ tsp fresh sage leaves (ground), some freshly ground black pepper, and ¼ tsp fresh hot pepper (seeds and all, ground together). Once the seasoning is mixed in, a small amount of sausage should be cooked to test for taste, and additions made as indicated.

Part of the sausage was made up into patties and wrapped separately for freezing; the rest was packed and frozen in 1-pound bags, except for some I kept out to combine with ground beef to make taco and enchilada fillings. (This combination is also good for spaghetti sauce and chili.)

Sesame or Benne

> *I take the liberty of sending you by Mr. Gallatin a bottle of salad oil, the first perhaps that was ever made in the United States. It was pressed from the seed of a plant which grows in the southern States, and is known there by the name of Bene.*
> —*Letter from W. Few to T. Jefferson, September 26, 1807*

CALL it Bene, Benne, Beni, Benni, Benney (all pronounced benny), or sesame, the seed was first brought to South Carolina by African slaves, who baked it in bread, boiled it with greens, and added it to broth. Jefferson considered it one of the most valuable acquisitions our country had made and thought it would eventually replace olive oil, butter, lard, and tallow.

Well, that it has not done, and it can't be produced as far north as he had hoped. But sesame seed makes a superlative oil for salads, sautéing, and baking and adds interest to a lot of dishes. Toasted sesame seed can be sprinkled on any type of roll or bread to add crunchy texture and flavor, it makes a good topping for casseroles, and Benne seed cookies are tops. Here are two types, both easy and excellent.

BENNE SEED DROP COOKIES. In bowl of mixer cream together ¾ C butter and 1½ C brown sugar. Add 2 eggs and mix at high speed until smoothly blended, then turn down speed and add 1 tsp vanilla and 1¼ C flour sifted with ¼ tsp baking powder. When smooth blend in ½ C toasted sesame seed. Drop by teaspoon on greased cookie sheet (allow room to spread) and bake until golden in moderate oven, about 350°. This makes a thin, crisp, delicious cookie.

For BENNE WAFERS mix ½ C butter and 1 C sugar (granulated); at high speed blend in 1 egg, ¼ C milk, and ½ tsp vanilla; turn back to slow speed and blend in 2 C flour sifted with ¼ tsp salt. When smooth, blend in ¾ C toasted sesame seed. Form dough into a roll about 1½ inches in diameter, wrap in plastic or foil, and chill. (At this stage the dough can be frozen for future use or kept in the refrigerator for several days.) Slice thin and bake on greased cookie sheet until golden in 375° oven.

I was reminded of benne seed because I've been doing some reading and thinking about "seed" lately—not the kind you plant but the seeds we eat, or don't eat. Did you know that recent research has proven that okra seed is higher in protein and nutrients than soybeans? I didn't, until I read about it. Heretofore I just tossed out okra pods that were too mature or dry to use fresh. Now I save the seed and add it to soups and casseroles and wonder why I never thought of doing it before.

Come to think of it, the seed of anything should contain a lot of nutrients. After all, it is the only source of food for the embryo in the seed, until the plant forms roots and derives nourishment from the soil.

Another thing that wonders me is why so many recipes call for removing the seed and pulp of tomatoes? If for some reason you have to steer clear of seedy dishes, do so, but otherwise there's no reason to discard this source of flavor, texture, and additional nutrition.

Going on this theory I've started using the seed from sweet peppers, tossing them into the salad instead of onto the compost heap. Even in sweet peppers the seed may be a bit pungent, but they're not really hot and they do add a certain zest to salads, soups, and casseroles.

Another thing that gets tossed out which could be utilized is corn shucks. These give the characteristic flavor to tamales, and it's easy as anything to dry your own. Select the outer green husks from ears of corn, dry for about a week, until they turn yellow, and then store in a brown paper bag. Before using them to wrap tamales, soak the dried shucks in warm water until they are pliable, then place in plastic bag to keep them soft. I am tempted to make up a big batch of tamales for the freezer, but this is one temptation I had better resist for the time being, considering everything else that has to be done in the next few days. For one thing, the first batch of Damson Conserve was so good that I got carried away and bought another big bag of damsons. And I'm still working on the eggplants, zukes, and tomatoes.

On one of the blessedly cool evenings last week, PASTA AND CHEESE seemed like a tempting idea for dinner but there wasn't space on the stove to make it the usual way, not to mention the fact that I was too tired to make a cream sauce base. My quickie version turned out so well I'll use it often from now on. After boiling and draining pasta shells I folded in some sour cream mixed with shredded sharp cheese and dumped it in a shallow baking dish, sprinkled on some more cheese, paprika, and ½ cup or so of wheat germ. Baked until it was bubbling, it was creamy, crusty, and just the right thing to round out the last slices of cold meat loaf.

This is still the Year of the Rabbit, but now we're coming into the Season of the Mouse. Deer, field, wood, pine, and meadow mice—and, for all I know, Mickey,

Hunca, and Munca—are all out there, getting ready for the annual invasion. In fact, some of their advance agents have already arrived. It is amazing how a single tiny mouse can, in certain situations, sound like an elephant.

The other morning Nancy Orme and I were comparing Mouse Tales, both our households having gone through several hours of murdered sleep the night before. (The Ormes live in a beautiful old stone house near Leesburg, but like all country houses—made of any material or of any vintage—it can't be made mouseproof.) The Orme mouse got cornered in a wastebasket (if a mouse can get "cornered" in a round container), and her husband, Sonny, eventually solved the problem by pouring water in the wastebasket. In our case the mouse ran in circles around a square closet, evading various missiles that were hurled at it. For what seemed like most of the night there was a recurring sound of gnawing, followed by the sound of a closet door opening, the thump of a shoe landing against the wall, silence, closet door closed, all quiet, everyone almost asleep, and then everything starting all over again. Finally one of the flung shoes hit on target and the invader was identified: one tiny mouse.

Recently we haven't had any resident cats to cope with the mouse problems. When we did, it was almost as unnerving to me as the mice themselves (and I must admit these little animals make me acutely uncomfortable), for the best hunter of the lot would catch a mouse but instead of doing anything decisive about it would go around for hours holding the mouse in her mouth—sort of like an all-day sucker—with the tail hanging out the side of her face.

Another amazing thing about mice is the way they can squinch up and get through what seem like impossibly small spaces—that is, when they are coming in. They don't seem to have the same ability when going out. One busy day before Christmas most of my time was spent trying to get a mouse out of a small pottery jar, a black Oaxacan pot I wanted to put some holly branches in. When I picked up the pot to fill it with water, the nose, whiskers, and one eye of a mouse popped up through the top. (I don't know which one of us was the more startled.) I couldn't bring myself to fill the pot with water and thus drown the mouse or float it out. It wouldn't shake out. Finally I hit on the idea of taking the pot outdoors, propping it on its side, and placing a tasty piece of cheese about three inches away from the opening. Success.

Jim Moran, who has made a career of doing and saying zany things that result in publicity, once observed that the greatest source of untapped energy in the world is Mouse Power. As he explained it, every time you see a mouse it is running somewhere, and to him it seems only reasonable to harness all this energy and put it to some useful purpose. After getting the latest bill for fuel oil I can only think, Oh, would that we could!

Goldenrod has been in bloom for over a month. More than twenty-five species of this handsome plant are found in this area. Some of them start blooming as early as July, while others flower into November. All of these and the various members of the tickseed family surely do light up the landscape, but there are a number of more modest flowers to be found now, if you look for them.

One of these is Gerardia, named for John Gerard, the herbalist. This is one of our native species, found nowhere else in the world, but seldom seen and admired as it deserves, since it comes at a season when there are so many larger, more flamboyant wildflowers to catch the attention.

The Gerardia is a foot or so tall on thin, wiry stems with needlelike leaves. The flowers, about an inch long and wide, are funnel shape, opening out to five broad petals. The throat is white, with tiny purple "freckles," and the rest of the flower is a beautiful lavender or pinkish purple.

When I go to buy stamps, which not only cost us more but seem to get bigger and more unattractive with each commemorative that comes out, I *wish* there could be some way to persuade the Postal Service to issue a comprehensive series of our native wildflowers. We are the only country in the world that does not have attractive wildflower stamps, and we are the only one with a number of these charming native flowers not found elsewhere which would make attractive stamps. This would be one way of making people aware of our rich botanical heritage, *and* it could certainly improve the appearance of our stamps.

A few that come to mind include Gerardia, dodecatheon (shooting star), Sabbatia (marsh pink), and phlox. Too, those like Jeffersonia, Lewisia, and Clarkia have additional reasons for being commemorated. Then when they ran out of flowers they could turn to birds, insects, and butterflies. I could give them enough ideas to use until the Tricentennial.

But then, nobody has asked me.

Girasoles or Jerusalem Artichokes

> *"Palestine soup!" said the Reverend Doctor Opimian, dining with his friend Squire Gryll; "a curiously complicated misnomer. We have an excellent old vegetable, the artichoke, of which we eat the head; we have another of subsequent introduction, of which we eat the root, and which we call artichoke because it resembles the first in flavour, although,* me judice, *a very inferior affair. This last is a species of the helianthus, or sunflower genus.... It is therefore a girasole, or turn-to-the-sun. From this girasole we have made Jerusalem, and from the Jerusalem artichoke we make Palestine soup."*
> —*Thomas Love Peacock,* Gryll Grange

THIS knobby little tuber with such distinctive flavor and interesting crisp texture has nothing to do with Jerusalem and it isn't an artichoke. It is a native sunflower, *Helianthus tuberosus,* and it was introduced to Europe in 1605 by the explorer Champlain, who found it being cultivated by the Indians on Cape Cod. The name Jerusalem is not a corrupt form of girasole, as has been suggested, but came from the fact that the plants reached London from Holland, where they were grown by Pastor Hondius at Terneuzen, and the artichoke *van Terneuzen* became artichokes of Jerusalem as the street hawkers cried them.

The tubers are clustered around the roots of the plant and are ready to harvest any time after the leaves begin to turn yellow. But unlike the potato, they should not all be harvested at once because they dry out so rapidly after being dug. If the ground over them is kept mulched, they may be dug as needed throughout the winter months.

The 1900 edition of Bailey's *Cyclopedia* emphasized their use for feeding hogs, by planting them and later turning the pigs in to root for them. Few people today would have a large enough crop to share with farm animals, but Annie Dilley says she feels like a truffle hound or hog when she roots around in the ground, trying to grub out all the tubers.

In Virginia a number of people raise enough for their own use, but on the West Coast they are now being cultivated commercially and from time to time are to be found in larger supermarkets, packaged under the name of Sun-Chokes. They may be served raw, steamed, sautéed, boiled, and baked; they are used in soups, stews, salads, and stir-fry dishes; and they make a marvelous crisp pickle or crunchy relish.

The first step in preparation is to scrub the tubers thoroughly. Betty Herbert has come up with the best idea yet for washing a big batch of them; she dumps them into the washing machine and lets them go through a wash and rinse cycle (*without* soap, I hasten to add). Kitty Lee Pritchett peels each one carefully—and this may be one of the reasons she makes her delicious pickle only every other year. They can also be scraped with a paring knife or rubbed with a plastic pot scrubber. Whatever method is used, they should be dropped immediately into cold water, with salt and a small amount of vinegar or lemon juice added to keep them from turning dark. Or, if a recipe calls for the tubers to be cooked, they may be parboiled and then the skin can be rubbed off easily with a piece of old terry towel or scraped off with a knife.

There is a wide choice of things to do with the cleaned tubers, starting out with GIRASOLE SALAD. Thinly sliced and marinated for a short while in French dressing, the 'chokes add an interesting flavor and texture to any tossed salad. Or they can be cooked until tender, peeled, cubed, dressed with a good mayonnaise, chilled, and served on lettuce.

Stir-fry cooks can add them to any recipes for Oriental dishes, including Eggs Foo Yong.

The PALESTINE SOUP served by Squire Gryll was a cream soup. To make it, coarsely chop 2 C 'chokes and cook in 2 C seasoned broth or water. When tender, put through food mill, add milk and cream to desired consistency, season to taste, add a lump of butter, heat, and serve. Or chill and serve with a spoonful of sour cream and some chopped parsley. When you boil Jerusalem artichokes for another purpose, save the salted broth, season to taste, and serve as a clear soup. Sliced or chopped 'chokes may be added to any vegetable soup or stew.

For BOILED 'CHOKES, cook until tender in salted water, just to cover, and rub off skin. Slice and serve with melted butter and seasoning. Or slice and add them to a light cream sauce, seasoned and sprinkled with grated cheese. Or put them through the food mill to make puree, add butter and a bit of cream, and season.

To make 'CHOKES AU GRATIN, precook as above, slice, place in a casserole in alternate layers with a rather thick cream sauce, add grated cheese to each layer, top with buttered crumbs, and bake until bubbling and browned on top.

Jerusalem artichokes can also be FRIED. Slice them thin and mix in a batter made of beaten egg and a small amount of oil and flour. Dip by spoonfuls into small amount of hot oil, fry on both sides until golden brown, drain, and garnish with fried parsley.

For SAUTEED 'CHOKES, slice, put into pan with small amount of butter, stir and cook until tender-crisp, season, garnish, and serve.

For BAKED 'CHOKES, parboil whole tubers, rub off skins, and add them to the pan juices of roasting beef or lamb about 30 minutes before meat will be done. Turn and baste in pan juices, just like browned potatoes.

ARTICHOKE RELISH. Most 'choke pickle and relish recipes call for the addition of mustard and turmeric. Here is the first of this type, an old recipe from South Carolina. Grind coarsely and mix 1 gallon of 'chokes, 12 sweet peppers (6 red, 6 green), 12 large onions, and 1 red hot pepper. Sprinkle with 2 C salt, cover, and let stand overnight in cool place. Next morning drain. Mix 4 C vinegar, 2 ounces dry mustard, 4 C granulated sugar, 1 ounce turmeric, 1 ounce celery seed, and 1 T mustard seed. Bring to boil, add drained vegetables, bring back to boil, pack in sterilized jars, and seal.

One summer I went over to Marshall to give a flower-arranging demonstration for the Upperville Garden Club. When we stopped to have a sandwich, Betty Herbert, one of the members, brought out a jar of the best 'choke pickles I had ever eaten. This brought up a discussion on the general subject of Jerusalem artichokes, and I ended up coming home with the pickles that were left, plus old family recipes from Betty and Kitty Lee Pritchett, another member. I never charge for doing these demonstrations, but I felt well paid that day.

Here are the recipes from Betty Herbert, different flavors, equally good. LIB'S ARTICHOKE PICKLE. Soak 1 peck of whole cleaned 'chokes overnight in 1 C salt and enough cold water to cover. Next morning fill quart jars ¾ full of 'chokes. Bring following mixture to rolling boil: 5 pounds granulated sugar, 3 pounds onions, sliced, 1 gallon vinegar, 1 regular box dry mustard, 1 T turmeric, and 6 small pods hot red pepper. Dip out onions first and divide evenly between jars, pour boiling juice over, and seal. The pickles will be ready to eat in a month.

For MITTIE'S ARTICHOKE PICKLE, soak 4 pounds scrubbed 'chokes in ½ gallon water and ¾ C salt for 3 hours. Combine 1 quart vinegar, 4 C sugar, 3 T celery seed, 3 T mustard seed, 2 T whole allspice, ½ ounce cinnamon sticks, 2 T whole cloves, and ¼ C tiny dried red peppers and boil for a few minutes. Drain 'chokes and mix with 3 medium onions, sliced. Pack into hot sterilized jars, cover with boiling-hot pickling juice, and seal. Makes about 7 pints.

The recipe from Kitty Lee came to Northern Virginia from Reidsville, North Carolina, by way of Danville. For this one, the 'chokes are scrubbed and peeled before being sliced and soaked in salt water. The original calls for soaking some of the vegetables and adding cucumbers and 'chokes on the second day, but it should work as well if all vegetables are mixed together at the same time.

SPECIAL ARTICHOKE PICKLE. Shred a large, firm head of cabbage, cover with cold water, and add about 1 C salt. Add the following to cabbage and let soak overnight: 2½ pounds onions, chopped; 2½ pounds small green tomatoes, sliced; 4 pounds 'chokes, peeled and sliced; 1 bunch of celery, sliced or chopped; 6 cucumbers, sliced; and 4 large green peppers, ground. Cover and place in a cool place.

Next morning bring to boil and drain immediately. Blend 1 ounce turmeric and 4 ounces dry mustard in ½ C olive oil until smooth. Add 1 T coarsely ground pepper, red pepper to taste, 1½ T celery seed, 2 pounds brown sugar, and 7 C vinegar. Bring to boil. Add drained vegetables, bring to boil again, and cook about 5 minutes. Stir in ¾ C flour dissolved in 1 C vinegar. Stir to blend thickening throughout mixture and seal in sterilized jars.

The Fourth Season

OCTOBER
Virginia Is for Apple Lovers

Few Planters but that have fair and large orchards, some of which have 1200 trees and upwards—bearing all sorts of English apples—of which they make great store of cider.
    —Thomas Glover, An Account of Virginia, 1676

THERE are only two species of apples native to this country, both crab apples, but desirable varieties were among the first plants brought by early settlers. As early as 1686 there was one orchard in Virginia with 2,500 grafted trees. In 1773, Jefferson's garden book records grafting Newtown Pippin in Albemarle County.

Even where there aren't written records, the large size and great age of seedling trees found about farm dwellings, on mountain slopes, in coves, and throughout the Great Valley indicate how early apples in this region were planted for home supply. A large number of varieties still commercially important originated here. Alas, some of the finer ones are no longer widely grown or easily found, including Bonum and Virginia Beauty.

In 1900, over 1,000 varieties were available for home planting. Now, most nurseries list no more than a dozen or so, and the main sources I know for obtaining stock of apples that are superior for dessert or eating are the New York State Fruit Testing Cooperative, in Geneva, New York 14456, which tests and introduces new fruits, and Henry Leuthardt, in East Moriches, New York 11940, who produces dwarf stocks of fine old varieties.

For cooking, of course, local roadside stands, markets, and orchards are spilling over with the new crop of apples for making sauce and butter, for baking and frying, and for turning into the best of all pies. Now is the time to buy apples in quantity and make the most of them.

When the air gets cool and crisp, who would settle for a cold cereal if he could trade for hot biscuits and FRIED APPLES? Certainly not anybody in this household. When I get up I start the coffee, get the bacon going, and set the oven. While the bacon is cooking I mix the biscuits and get them ready to go into the oven. When the bacon is done, I pour off all but about 3 or 4 T of remaining fat, dump in apples (5 or 6) that have been cored and sliced, add a pinch of salt, cover, and cook on fairly high heat for about 5 minutes. By this time the oven is ready for the biscuits.

Turn and stir the apples, add brown sugar ($\frac{1}{2}$ to $\frac{3}{4}$ C), and cover to continue cooking. In another 5 minutes uncover the apples, stir, add a little water if they are too dry, and cook a bit longer. All told, this takes about 30 minutes, and nobody has to be called twice for breakfast.

Another mainstay is applesauce, both canned and frozen. It is so good as is, and so many things can be made with it: cake, muffins, cookies, etc. Frozen applesauce, served before it is completely thawed, is like a sherbet, and canned applesauce that is chilled and topped with whipped cream makes an elegant dessert.

For APPLESAUCE, core and quarter apples, barely cover with water, and cook until soft. Put through food mill and add sugar and desired spice to taste. Freeze or pack into sterilized jars, seal, and process 5 minutes at 10 pounds pressure.

For APPLESAUCE CAKE, beat in a mixer 1 C

brown sugar, ½ C shortening, and 1 egg. When this is fluffy, add alternately 1 C thick sweetened applesauce and these sifted dry ingredients: 1¾ C cake flour, ½ tsp salt, 1 tsp each soda and cinnamon, ½ tsp cloves, and 2 T cocoa. When blended fold in 2 C chopped nuts. Bake in tube pan for 40 minutes at 350°.

APPLESAUCE PUDDING is light and delicious. Separate 3 eggs. Beat the whites with a pinch of salt, 6 T sugar, and desired flavoring and set aside. In another bowl beat together 3 C sweetened applesauce, the egg yolks, grated lemon rind, and about 2 tsp of the juice. Fold in about ⅓ of meringue mixture, pour into soufflé dish, and top with rest of meringue. Set dish in shallow pan of water and bake in 300° oven until light brown. Good hot or cold.

I suppose there are as many ways of making APPLE PIE as there are moms. I've tried a lot of them, but here is our favorite. Whether you're a beginner or an old hand, PASTE CRUST is the easiest kind to make and it is the best for any fruit pie. Mix ⅔ C sifted flour with ¼ C water to make a paste. In another bowl mix 1⅓ C sifted flour and 1 tsp salt and blend in ⅔ C shortening. Add paste, blend, and turn with your hands until it makes a smooth ball. Chill in refrigerator for 1 hour. While this is chilling, prepare apples.

Rinse, remove rind, and dice two ¼-inch slices of fatback (yes, *fatback*). Render until crisp and set aside. Peel, core, and slice 6 large apples and mix with 1 C sugar, ⅛ tsp cinnamon, and ⅛ tsp freshly ground nutmeg. Roll out crust and line a 9-inch pan (I use an old Pennsylvania Dutch earthenware pie plate, and I swear it makes a difference). Pour in apple mixture, cover with crisp pork and fat, put on top crust, and bake for 10 minutes at 400°; then turn heat back to 350° and bake for another 30 or 40 minutes. I know it sounds crazy—but try it, you'll like it.

ROSY APPLES is a sweet salad the youngsters always expect with a holiday feast. Pare, core, and quarter or slice 4 large apples. Slowly cook and baste in a syrup made of 1 C water, ½ C sugar, and ¼ C red-hots or cinnamon drops. When apples are tender, chill in syrup. Serve cold, in lettuce cups, topped with cream cheese that has been softened with cream.

After watching me make strudel dough, the children renamed this one "APPLE STRUGGLE," but now you can buy packages of strudel dough, all rolled out, ready to fill and bake. Pare, core, and thinly slice 3 pounds apples; mix with ½ C sugar, 1 tsp cinnamon, and ⅓ C each slivered almonds and raisins. Lightly brown ¾ C fine bread crumbs in ½ C butter, spread over ⅔ of the prepared strudel dough, and cover with the apple mixture. Gently roll over and over, pinching together seams and ends. Slide onto baking sheet, brush with melted butter, and bake in hot (about 400°) oven for 45 minutes or until golden brown. Dust with powdered sugar and serve warm or cold. (This filling may be enough to fill two or three of the commercial strudel leaves; just divide and proceed accordingly.)

APPLE BREAD is extremely good, spread with cream cheese for tea or with a fruit salad and soup for lunch (either served at home or packed in a lunch box). In mixer blend ¼ C shortening, ⅔ C sugar, and 2 eggs until light and fluffy. Sift together 2 C flour and 1 tsp each baking powder, soda, and salt. Add alternately to first mixture with 2 C coarsely shredded apples. At last, stir in 1 T grated lemon rind and ⅔ C chopped nuts. Bake in standard loaf pan at 350° for about an hour, or until it tests done. Do not slice until cold.

APPLE MUFFINS really round out a bowl of homemade vegetable soup, and nothing is more filling and satisfying on a cold, dreary day. In ⅔ C milk, soak 1¼ C whole bran for a few minutes. Add 2 eggs, 1 C sugar, and ¼ C cooking oil and beat until well blended. Sift together 1 C flour, 2 tsp baking powder, ½ tsp salt, and ¼ tsp each cinnamon and cloves. Quickly mix with other ingredients and fold in 1 C each finely chopped apples and raisins. Bake about 25 minutes in hot (400°) oven.

APPLE CRISP or crunch is a quick and easy dessert to make while you're cooking dinner. Peel, core, and thinly slice enough apples to make a 2-inch layer in a square cake pan. Blend, with fingers, ¾ C rolled oats, ¾ C brown sugar, ½ C flour, ¼ tsp salt, and ½ C butter. Sprinkle over apples and bake in 375° oven for about 30 minutes. Serve hot or warm, with cream.

APPLE CANDY is very good and doesn't contain any preservatives or other junk that goes into commercial candy. Cook enough applesauce to make 2 C of fairly thick pulp. Add 2 C sugar and a pinch of salt. Continue to cook slowly until it is thick and sheets from a spoon. Meanwhile, soften 2 envelopes of gelatin in ⅔ C cold water. Add to hot pulp, stirring to dissolve. When mixture begins to cool, stir in 1½ C walnut meats and ¼ tsp each of orange and vanilla extracts (or substitute grated orange rind for the extract). Pour into pan that has been coated with some nonstick product. When firm and cold, cut into squares and roll in powdered sugar.

For APPLE BUTTER, remove stems, quarter apples, and cook until tender in enough cider to not quite cover. Put through food mill. To each C of pulp add ½ C sugar, 2 tsp cinnamon, 1 tsp cloves, ½ tsp allspice, ½ tsp grated lemon rind, and 1 tsp lemon juice. Cook in enamel preserving kettle, first over low heat, stirring constantly until sugar is dissolved; then cook fairly rapidly, stirring frequently, until it sheets from a spoon. Or place a small spoonful on a saucer; when no rim of liquid separates around the edge, the butter is done. Pour into sterilized jars and seal.

When you use pared apples in any recipe, don't discard the peelings; use them to make APPLE JELLY. Cover apple peelings and cores with water, cook until soft, and strain. To each cupful of juice add ¾ C sugar and boil until it reaches jelly stage. Pour immediately into sterilized jelly glasses and cover with paraffin. For a delicate-flavored jelly that is different you can put a rose, lemon, or peppermint geranium leaf in the bottom of the glass before pouring in the jelly. Or make a MINT JELLY by cooking fresh mint leaves with the jelly and adding a small amount of green coloring.

Of course there are many other ways to use apples—in

pancakes, dumplings, Waldorf salad; made into chutneys and catsups; preserved, scalloped, poached. They're good served raw with cheese or combined with other fruits. And nothing tops them for eating out of hand (that is, unless you've reached that biblical stage in life "when the grinders are gone").

In addition to everything else, they can be made into dolls. Peeled and dried (without cutting out the core), slices of them turn into puckery, funny little "faces" that can be made into charming little figures.

Those early settlers certainly started something when they brought the first apple trees to Virginia. Of course they came and prospered in other areas too, but so many good apples originated here and are now being produced and shipped in quantity that it doesn't seem too prejudiced to say that Virginia *is* for apple lovers—everywhere.

Of Pepo, Pompion, Punkin, Pumpkin

The fruit is of a great bigneff, whofe barke is full of little bunnies or hillie welts . . . which is yellow when it is ripe.
—Gerard's Herbal, *"The Great Round Pompion"*

FROM now through Halloween and on until Thanksgiving, the Great Round Pompion should be a familiar sight, stacks of them for sale at just about every roadside market and fruit stand. And wherever you see a pile of pumpkins there will most likely be a passel of young'uns, picking and choosing just the right one to make a jack-o'-lantern.

From Cinderella's coach to Linus's annual vigil in the pumpkin patch, this round, golden fruit (or vegetable) is associated with fun, traditions, and special celebrations. It appears over and over in fairy tales, nursery rhymes, poems, and the sort of ghost stories that make you want to jump into bed and pull the covers over your head.

Wherever and whenever the custom started, children continue to carve jolly faces in pumpkin shells, most of

Of Pepo, Pompion, Punkin, Pumpkin / 165

them simple cutouts for eyes, nose, and a toothy grin. However, in a few parts of England children celebrate Punkie Night, for which the punkie or pumpkin is carved with intricate scenes or designs: houses, horses, dogs, ships, or flowers. Most of the pulp is carefully scooped out, leaving just a thin layer of meat to support the shell. With a lighted candle inside, these designs become transparencies and the pumpkin lanterns glow with a warm, golden light of fascinating patterns.

Simple or intricate, crude or carved with skill, the homemade punkin lantern is infinitely superior to a plastic copy of the real thing. It not only looks more interesting and attractive but is safer, from the standpoint of fire hazard, *and* the scooped-out pulp and seeds can be put to good use. For from seeds to shell, soup to nuts, the Great Round Pompion is a treat to eat.

In 1607 John Smith found the Indians in Virginia growing pompions with their corn. They cooked the pumpkin in a "broth," mixed it with ground corn for a sort of pudding or porridge, made it into bread, and dried the pulp for winter use. Even earlier than this the pompion was known and grown in Europe. The fruit, "boyled in milke and buttered," was not only considered good but, being so prepared, was said to bring relief to "such as have a hot stomache or the inward parts inflamed." The flesh or pulp, sliced and fried in butter, was also considered to be wholesome, but when baked with apples was thought to fill the body with "flatuous or windie belchings" and be utterly unwholesome for "such as live idelly." An exception noted that "unto robustious and rustick people, nothing hurteth that filleth the belly."

By the early part of the nineteenth century in this country there was a lively exchange of seeds and information on the pompion, which was now called pumpkin. There was interest in finding more productive strains which could be used for feeding workhorses, cattle, and sheep and as the principal fattening for hogs, in addition to those of fine flavor and thick meat for table use.

Since the pumpkin is native to the warmer parts of

Africa and Asia, as well as tropical America, it is interesting to compare the similarities and differences in the way it is used in different countries. In some places the leaves of the plant are cooked, much like spinach; the seeds are toasted and eaten just about everywhere; some African dishes combine pumpkin with cornmeal in a porridge that is probably similar to the way the Indians cooked it; the pumpkin empanada of Mexico is a sister-under-the-skin to New England pie; and there are versions of soup ranging from a delicate broth with tender-crisp bits of pumpkin to creamy blends including other vegetables. Here are some of the less usual but equally good ways to prepare *Cucurbita pepo*, the Great Round Pompion.

Start with the PUMPKIN SEEDS; no matter what you plan to do with the rest of the pumpkin, by all means save the seeds. When toasted they are delicious eaten out of hand or used to replace nuts in various recipes. To prepare, just separate unwashed pumpkin seeds from fiber and to each 2 C of seeds add 1½ T butter or oil and 1½ tsp coarse salt. Spread on a cookie sheet and bake in 250° oven, stirring occasionally, until crisp and brown.

CREAMY PUMPKIN SOUP is good no matter how it's served, but for a festive occasion try serving it in a tureen made from its own shell. Select a pumpkin of adequate size and nice shape, being sure to get one with some stem, which will be the handle on the lid. After cutting out the lid, remove fiber and seeds and then carefully scoop out pulp, leaving the shell about ½ inch thick. (A cheese scoop, melon ball cutter, and sharp-edge spoon will all be helpful in scooping out the meat.)

For each 4 C of chopped pumpkin pulp allow 1 medium onion, 1 large potato, 2 medium tomatoes (all peeled and chopped), and 1 quart of broth or water. Wilt onion in small amount of butter; add chopped vegetables and broth or water. Season with coarse salt, freshly ground pepper, a dash or two of Tabasco, some celery leaves, and fresh parsley. Cook until vegetables are soft, put them through the food mill, add a lump of butter and enough cream to give desired consistency, and adjust seasonings to taste. Heat and serve with crisp croutons.

There are a lot of recipes for pumpkin bread but here is a PUMPKIN BUTTER, which makes a good spread on any type of bread. Grind about 6 C of firm pumpkin chunks and add 4 C light brown sugar and juice and grated rind of 1 fresh lemon. Stir, cover, and let stand overnight. Next morning add 1 C orange juice and cook and stir over low heat until it is thick.

For those Mexican versions of the pumpkin pie, try PUMPKIN EMPANADAS. For filling, combine 1 C pumpkin pulp with ½ C each chopped almonds and white raisins, ¼ C sugar, ¼ tsp salt, and 1 tsp coriander seed. Cook over low heat until thick, then cool.

Roll out a short pie crust (either your own or a mix) fairly thin and cut into 4-inch circles. Put a spoonful of cooled filling on one side, dampen edges, fold and seal, and bake until light brown in a hot oven; while hot, sprinkle with powdered sugar and cinnamon.

Of course PUMPKIN SHELLS can be used for purposes other than culinary. They are the traditional place for "keeping" wives (as in "Peter, Peter, Pumpkin Eater"), if you're of a certain age you will remember that a pumpkin shell provided the hiding place for microfilms of the famous Pumpkin Papers, and they make amusing and interesting "containers" for arrangements of fall flowers. (Just put a piece of damp oasis in an empty pumpkin shell and stick in a great splodge of chrysanthemums of all colors—instant effect!)

Last week I spent several days in the four-poster with "whatever it is that's going around." Misery doesn't *always* love company. I was miserable and I sure didn't want any company—especially not one particular "guest."

There I was, propped up on pillows, halfway between reading and dozing off, when I heard a sort of rustling sound. I looked around, saw nothing, and went back to reading. The noise continued so I looked more closely. It seemed absurd but the carvings on the bedpost, right by my head, looked as if they were changing position and moving around. I accept the fact that I'm myopic and I knew I was feverish but this manifestation seemed passing peculiar.

When I got close enough to see what it was, it seemed to be too close. There I was, eye to eye with a snake. It was a rather charming snake and looked very decorative against the background of carved rosewood, but I had no guarantee that it would stay there.

After having a relatively brief debate with myself, one of us decided that something had to be done about the situation! First, I apologized to the snake, saying, "I *wish* you hadn't done this." Then, covering my hand with a Kleenex (and what possible protection that might have been against a snakebite is beyond me; it just seemed like a good idea at the time) I grabbed the snake just behind the head and carried it outside. At first I intended just to let it go; then it occurred to me that if it got in once it could get back in again, or where there was one, there might be more, and it might be a good idea for me to know whether and which. So with decidedly mixed feelings I killed the little creature, and I'm still sorry I had to do it.

Not just the color but also the pattern changed once it was dead. Not being sure of identification, I put it in a jar of alcohol and passed it along to an expert. It was a black rat snake, which is probably the same species as the other black snakes we have in more-or-less residence around the place. Markings change as they mature and precise identification depends on getting close enough to examine their scales (closer than I plan to get), but as I understand it the black rat snake differs mainly from the black racer, the other type of black snake found hereabouts, in that the former climbs and the latter doesn't.

They're both helpful snakes and good to have around —just *not around the bedpost when I'm in the bed.*

Pawpaws, 'Simmons, and Such

*Sich pop-paws!—Lumps o' raw Gold and green, jes'
oozy th'ough With ripe yaller, like you've saw Custard pie with no crust to.*
                            —James Whitcomb Riley, "Armazindy"

SINCE Xerox bought the land across the way and put up Trespassers William signs all over the place, my favorite, in fact only, pawpaw patch is off limits. This northern cousin of the tropical custard apple tribe—including pond apple, soursop, sweetsop, sugar apple, and papaya—should be found growing in numerous colonies hereabouts; I just haven't found them.

If this is an acquired taste, I must have acquired it early on, for I can remember as a small child going to the country and looking for pawpaws, eating all I could hold and bringing home all I could carry. (Even as a young'un my dresses had to have large pockets, for putting things in. And those pleated bloomers we wore, *pour le sport*, may have looked like a modest skirt, but each leg, gathered in with elastic, provided a sizable pouch for toting home green apples, pawpaws, or other interesting items collected in the woods or along the waysides.)

Where available, pawpaws were a staple of the Indians' diet, and they were about the only thing the Lewis and Clark expedition had to eat when they got back as far as Missouri, with game scarce and supplies running out.

They have to be ripe to develop the unusual flavor, somewhere between mango and banana. On the farm they were put in the haymow or bran bin to "mellow." Lacking these facilities, one could wrap them in a scrap of old quilt or blanket and store in a drawer until ripe. Now is the time to be on the lookout for pawpaws, in open woodlands or along streams.

More easily found are the native persimmons, which grow in fields and fencerows or along the edge of woods.

There are occasional trees that bear sweet fruit, even before frost, but to be on the safe side collect the fruit after frost, or put it in the freezer to get mellow, for a " 'Simmon, Green Persimmon" sure can pucker your mouth. Once ripe, however, these "soft sugar lumps of fruit" are delicious to eat as is, and they make excellent bread, cake, pudding, and a marvelous milkshake. Good things (or should I say interesting things) have been said for persimmon beer; having never tried it I can't give a first-hand report on this.

PERSIMMON CAKE. At high speed mix 1 C sugar with ½ C soft butter until light and fluffy. Turn down speed and blend in 1 C persimmon pulp. Add 1¾ C sifted cake flour, resifted with 1 tsp each soda and cinnamon and ½ tsp each salt and cloves, and blend until smooth. Fold in 1 C chopped nuts (hickory nuts for first choice but pecans are almost as good). Bake in buttered and floured 9-inch tube pan for about 40 minutes at 350°.

PERSIMMON BREAD. At high speed blend ¼ C vegetable oil with ½ C brown sugar and 1 egg. Turn down speed and blend in 1 C persimmon pulp. Add alternately 1 C buttermilk and dry mixture consisting of 1½ C sifted white flour, ½ tsp salt, 1 tsp soda, and 1½ C whole wheat flour. When smooth, fold in 1 C chopped walnuts. Bake in 1 large or 2 small bread pans for about 1¼ hours at 350°. Let cool in pan before turning out, and chill in refrigerator a few hours before slicing.

PERSIMMON PUDDING is a light steamed pudding with a delicate flavor, less spicy than the foregoing recipes. At high speed mix 1 C sugar with 2 egg yolks, ¼ C bland oil, and 2 T brandy until well blended and light. Turn down speed and add 1½ C bread crumbs mixed with 2 tsp baking powder and 1 C milk. When smooth, fold in 2 stiffly beaten egg whites and 1 C persimmon pulp. Spoon mixture into buttered pudding mold or recycled tin cans, cover with aluminum foil, and steam: about 2 hours in a steamer, or 30 minutes at 15 pounds in a pressure pan. Serve with sweetened, flavored whipped cream or a simple sauce.

SIMPLE PUDDING SAUCE. Combine ¼ C sugar with 1 T cornstarch and 1 C water. Cook and stir over medium heat until thick and translucent. Remove from heat stir in 2 or 3 T butter and a pinch of salt. Flavor to taste with brandy, rum, or any suitable liqueur, or flavor with the rind and juice of lemon or orange.

No wild fruits are sweeter than ripe black haw, and they make a delicious jelly or syrup. This shrub or small tree, along with the other sweet viburnums—nannyberry and the withe rods—grows all around this area. We have quantities of the bushes here on the place, but the birds and squirrels usually get to them first. Now is also the time to hunt for wild grapes and other edible berries, including red-fruited barberry, mountain ash, and the hips of sweetbrier rose.

The custard apple in the first paragraph reminded me of a request for a recipe for baked custard pie "like grandmother used to make." Well, there are a number of ways to make custard pie. Not knowing which one "grandmother" used, I passed along an old Southern recipe, since this particular grandmother came from North Carolina.

BUTTERMILK CUSTARD PIE. Mix at high speed 3 egg yolks, 1½ C sugar, and 7 T very soft butter. When smooth, turn down speed and blend in 4 T sifted flour; then at very low speed mix in 2 C buttermilk. Fold in egg whites that have been beaten until stiff.

Pour into hot, partially baked shell, turn oven heat down to 300°, and bake pie for 30 minutes. (Nobody knows why, but this one tastes very much like coconut custard and is not only different but delicious.)

This week when I stopped by a roadside stand to get some late corn, a basket of big, blocky peppers was brought in, fresh from the field. They were priced right, so I got two dozen to stuff and put in the freezer.

Of course just about anything can be used to stuff peppers, but for these I used rice, with some onion, fresh corn, tomatoes, fresh herbs, and the last bits of a ham chopped into bite-size chunks. There was enough filling left over to add some chopped pepper and serve for lunch, so I put all the stuffed peppers in the freezer. Packed in bake-and-serve containers, they can go right from the freezer to the oven, with only the addition of some cheese or buttered crumbs for topping. This is the sort of thing that is good to have on hand for times when you're too tired or otherwise not inclined to start dinner from scratch.

Last night I was too tired, and definitely not inclined, but there was a fresh bluefish, split for broiling, so I started from scratch! My fish-broiling method is somewhat unorthodox—sort of off again, on again, requiring a minimum of oil or butter; the fish comes out moist, with a delicate flavor and tempting aroma. For BROILED BLUEFISH, place the flattened-out fish on a nonstick baking sheet, skin side down. Brush lightly with oil or dot with tiny bits of butter; sprinkle with coarse salt, freshly ground pepper, juice of fresh lime or lemon, and paprika; and top off with some fresh herbs. (This time I used fresh rosemary leaves and some sprigs of thyme.)

Place in cold oven, on rack about 3 inches from broiler, close door, and then turn heat to broil. As soon as fish starts to smoke and sputter, turn off the heat and leave the oven door closed. After a few minutes turn the heat on again and repeat as above. It may take two or three of these cycles, depending on thickness of fish. With this method there is no need to turn or baste the fish, and it comes out moist but nicely browned. This is one thing paprika does; it gives a good browned surface to roasted, baked, or broiled poultry and fish.

My snake-on-the-bedpost piece brought some interesting responses. One reader reported on a snake incident during the Waterford Fair. One of the workers was quietly sitting in a pew in the Presbyterian church when a big black snake lost its footing, or its equilibrium, or whatever a snake loses when it falls. Anyhow, it slipped from a beam overhead, came plummeting down, and landed right in her lap. Don't know whether she was meditating or just resting, but it sure broke her train of thought.

Mrs. Lyon was reminded of the time she came home from a garden club meeting to find the front hall sealed off, with all doors tightly shut. Explanation? A black snake was somewhere in the hall. Eventually it was located, firmly wrapped around the finial of the grandfather clock. Efforts to dislodge it gently, or disengage it from the finial with long-handled tree pruners, only made it constrict and wind more tightly and the clock rock more perilously. Finally, Mr. Lyon had to "prune" it, so to speak, and amputate it from the clock.

By far the funniest and most ingenious solution for snake removals came from our friend Sarah Douglass, who was at home, alone, when she discovered a black snake in an upstairs bedroom. Not wanting to touch it with her hand, nor having a forked stick handy, she did some quick thinking, grabbed the vacuum cleaner, took off the brush, and sucked the snake up through the hose into the cleaner bag. Then she stopped up the end of the hose and took cleaner, snake, and all outside for her husband, Ned, to cope with when he returned home.

While I had Sarah on the line I persuaded her to part with her recipe for spoon bread—somewhat different from the many others I've tried and certainly the best of the lot. SARAH'S SPOON BREAD. With a hand mixer beat 4 egg whites until stiff and set aside. In a large saucepan bring 4 C sweet milk just to the boil; then, again using hand mixer, stir constantly while slowly adding 1 C white cornmeal. When mixture is smooth remove from heat and, continuing to beat, add 1 stick of butter, 2 T sugar, 1 tsp salt, and the beaten yolks of 4 eggs. Finally, fold in stiffly beaten egg whites and turn batter into buttered casserole or deep dish. Place on middle rack of oven preheated to 350°, with shallow pan of hot water on bottom rack. Bake until puffed and light brown, about 45 minutes.

Providing this steam during the baking makes all the difference in the texture of this spoon bread variation. I always use this steam method when baking my Quick Crusty Bread or French Bread, but I had never once thought of trying it with other things. Sarah says it is not only good for baking the spoon bread originally but great for heating up any that might be left over, and she also bakes corn pudding the same way.

Her vacuum cleaner solution never occurred to me during my own snake crisis, but come to think of it I did resort to the vacuum cleaner one winter when some wasps or hornets got activated in the attic. Whatever they were, they were angry and coming on strong, numerically as well as otherwise. Swatting them one by one wasn't very effective or very safe, but when I got the cleaner revved up it was easy enough to scoop them up as they emerged; I just had to spend all day manning the battle station.

If I can just remember, the next time someone from the city asks me what I find to *do* all day out here in the country, I can say, "Oh, I catch hornets in the vacuum cleaner, unwind snakes from the bedpost—all the usual things that anybody does with her time."

NOVEMBER
Game Plan for Feasts

And a-hunting we will go.
—Henry Fielding

WHEN we lived down at Abingdon, Jim did a good bit of bird hunting and fairly frequently, during the season, we had quail, or "potridge," as some people down there call it. Usually we just roasted the birds with a bit of bacon across the breast and served them with great bowls of fresh watercress from the nearby stream.

Once he bagged a ruffed grouse, which Chuckie, our cook of the moment, prepared. After putting some herbs in the cavity she seasoned the bird, put it, with a little broth, in a close-fitting tin (tightly covered), and placed it on the rack of our large canning kettle, half filled with water. Once it came to a boil she let it simmer along until it was done. I don't know how she timed it or how much of what she put with it, but after being cooked and chilled and slipped out of the tin it was encased in a layer of shimmering jelly. Easily the best bird-and-bottle feast we have ever had.

After coming out to "the forty acres" we found that it just wasn't possible to kill or eat game from the place. Who could shoot a wild turkey when it brings its babies right up on the terrace to strut around and show them off? Or a deer that pauses at the kitchen window and peers in to watch you washing dishes? Or quail that hatch their young in the shrubs by the house, then bring them around to be fed? Or rabbits that regularly come to the French doors and act like they're just waiting to be let in? Or even the pesky muskrats! They wreck the dam at the end of the pond, but we couldn't lay a finger on them after watching an industrious mama forage for grass along the shore, swimming back to her den on the island with a pile of grass on her back that would be comparable to my carrying a haystack. So I haven't cooked any game for some time, but I haven't forgotten how it's done.

Cooking game is about as far as you can get from bland, plastic-wrapped, heat-and-serve fare. First you have to bag it, hang it, skin, pluck, clean, dress—whatever—and in some cases let it marinate for several days before you even start cooking it. Is the finished product worth the effort? Beyond question. The following recipes are based on the premise that you have "caught your possum" and done the advance preparation. Limits of space prevent including the whole operation from buckshot to bird-in-oven.

A marinade, which tenderizes and adds flavor and aroma, may be as simple as a mixture of vinegar and water with a few spices tossed in, but a combination of wine or cider vinegar, herbs, spices, and some vegetables is even better. Here are two marinades that give a general idea of basic proportions and procedures.

WHITE MARINADE. To 4 C cider and ½ C white vinegar add 2 onions, 2 carrots, and 2 shallots (coarsely chopped); sprigs of thyme, parsley, rosemary, and a bay leaf; 5 peppercorns and 5 juniper berries; and 2 tsp salt. Bring to boil and cook for about 5 minutes.

RED MARINADE. In a small amount of oil brown 2 onions, 2 carrots, 2 garlic cloves, and 2 celery ribs with leaves, all coarsely chopped. Add 2 C red wine, 1½ C wine vinegar, 2 tsp salt, 6 juniper berries, whole allspice, and peppercorns. Boil for about 5 minutes.

After a marinade has been cooked to release flavors, it must be thoroughly chilled before pouring over the meat. Enclose meat and marinade in a heavy plastic bag, tie the top, and place the bag in a bowl or pan to catch any drips. Keep in refrigerator, turning the bag from time to time. Use fresh juniper berries if available—our Virginia cedars are a good source for an abundant supply. If a marinade doesn't cover the meat, just add enough extra wine or cider and vinegar to do the job.

Tender venison can be roasted—at about the same time and temperature required for beef—and the steaks may be pan-broiled or grilled. Venison also makes an excellent ragout or stew, but for something special try BRAISED VENISON. Marinate a haunch or ¾-inch steaks for 2 days. Remove meat, wipe dry, and brown in a small amount of oil or bacon drippings. Add marinade, cover, and cook in a moderate oven until meat is tender. Thicken sauce if necessary, put through food mill, and serve over meat. For vegetables, serve red cabbage and brown lentils.

Various tart jellies go well with venison, but the classic accompaniment is CUMBERLAND SAUCE. Cook together for 3 or 4 minutes 1 C currant jelly and the grated rind and juice of 1 lemon and 1 orange. Add ½ C port. Thicken with 2 tsp cornstarch dissolved in water, stir, and cook until clear. Cool before serving. The addition of 1 T Grand Marnier improves the flavor. (Red wine may be substituted for the port, in which case add sugar to taste.)

Rabbit can be fried, stewed, or baked like chicken, but HASENPFEFFER is even better. Cut rabbit in serving pieces and marinate for 2 days in the Red Marinade. Remove, pat dry, dredge with flour, and brown in a small amount of butter or bacon drippings. Strain marinade and add 2 C of the juice to meat. Cover and bake in moderate oven 1 hour or so. Thicken gravy with a small amount of flour and add salt and pepper to taste.

For quail or partridge with a different flavor try VINE-WRAPPED QUAIL. Rub the inside cavity of the dressed bird with butter and salt, tuck in a sprig of oregano, sprinkle the outside of the bird with freshly ground pepper, and wrap it in 2 or 3 vine leaves, held in place with a strip of bacon. (Vine leaves, preserved in brine, are available in some supermarkets as well as in Greek groceries.) Roast in an open pan at 350° or simmer in broth in a covered pan, about 30 minutes. Instead of wild rice (always high, now out of sight), try brown rice, hominy grits, sprouted rye, or bulgur (cracked wheat). All are great with game birds.

When roasting a goose, remember to cook it on a rack in an open pan and prick the skin frequently to release excess fat.

I lay claim to no expertise at cooking wild duck, but from conflicting instructions in some "authentic" recipes found in a regional cookbook it would appear that cooking a wild duck is like skinning a cat—more than one way of doing it. One recipe says, "Soak ducks 24 hours in salted water"; another cautions, "Don't put ducks in water, just wipe with a damp rag." One calls for stuffing the duck as full as possible with uncut celery stalks; another says, "Do not stuff with *anything*." The entire cooking time ranges from 20 minutes to ½ hour or a bit longer. The addition of liquids to the roasting pan varies from none at all to filling the cavity with brandy and wine at half time and basting with more brandy and wine as cooking continues. (You might call this one Drunken Duck, and serve Tipsy Pudding for dessert!)

However you cook waterfowl, there *is* a trick to getting it disengaged from its feathers. If it isn't plucked dry, add some detergent to the boiling water in which it is dipped. Then, to remove any remaining pinfeathers, coat with a warm mixture of half beeswax and half paraffin. When this wax coating cools it can be peeled off and the pinfeathers will come with it.

Great Native Nuts

And, close at hand, the basket stood
With nuts from brown October's wood.
        —John Greenleaf Whittier, "Snowbound"

SHAGBARK, shellbark, mockernut—all the sweet and edible hickories are among the best of our native nuts, but there are doubtless many people today who have never even tasted one, and you won't find recipes calling for them except in very old cookbooks or collections of family recipes.

The shelled nutmeats *may* be found in some farmers' markets. Every year, around Thanksgiving, Mother used to send me about five pounds of the shelled nuts of the big shellbarks that grow in the Ohio Valley. What a treat! Now the only way I know to get hickory nuts is to spot a tree and get there first, before the squirrels.

If you see a very tall tree with unusually rich golden fall foliage, it is probably a hickory. The shagbarks and mockernuts are more usually found in this area, but the red hickory also grows hereabouts. This one has small nuts, not much over 1 inch long including hull, but both husk and shell are thin and the nuts are delicious.

Just in case you're lucky (or energetic) enough to have hickory nuts, here are four interesting ways to use them. Pecans (which are in the same family) can be substituted, but they won't taste the same. Note that none of these recipes calls for vanilla or other additional flavoring; the hickory nut flavor is the thing.

HICKORY NUT CAKE NO. 1. Cream together until light and fluffy ⅔ C soft butter and 2 C sugar. Add 3 egg yolks and beat until smooth. Add 1 C milk alternately with 2¼ C sifted cake flour which has been resifted with 2¼ tsp baking powder. When smooth, fold in 2 egg whites which have been beaten until stiff with a pinch of salt. Finally, fold in 1 C chopped hickory nuts. Bake in 2 layer pans, about 25 minutes at 350°. Turn out to cool on racks. Before serving, fill with sweetened whipped cream and sprinkle top of cake with powdered sugar.

HICKORY NUT CAKE NO. 2. Cream together 1 C soft butter and 2 C sugar until light and fluffy. Add 2 egg yolks and beat until smooth. Add 1 C milk alternately with dry mixture of 2¾ C sifted cake flour, sifted with 2 tsp cream of tartar and 1 tsp soda. Fold in 5 egg whites stiffly beaten with pinch of salt. Finally, fold in 2 C chopped hickory nuts that have been mixed with ¼ C sifted cake flour. Bake in tube pan or layers, filling and/or topping with seven-minute icing.

HICKORY NUT CUSTARD makes a marvelous filling for a basic butter cake, baked in layers. Combine 2 C milk 1 T cornstarch, 2 eggs, ½ C sugar, and 2 C chopped hickory nuts. Cook and stir on very low heat or in a double boiler until thick and smooth. Remove from heat and stir occasionally until lukewarm. Spread between layers of cake; then chill before serving. The top of the cake can be sprinkled with powdered sugar or spread with whipped cream.

HICKORY NUT COOKIES were always my favorite —crisp and crinkly on top with a delectable flavor. Blend together 2 C sugar, 2 eggs, ½ C melted butter, and 6 T milk until smooth. Add 1 C flour sifted with 1 tsp cream of tartar and ½ tsp soda. When smooth, stir in 1 C chopped hickory nuts and, finally, blend in enough additional flour to make a soft dough. Drop by teaspoons on a greased cookie sheet (allowing room to spread) and bake at 375° until golden brown.

Anna Hedrick called to say the piece on pawpaws brought back happy memories of an annual event when she was growing up. On the first Sunday in October her father always led a family expedition out along the Potomac to collect pawpaws. This sort of outing was fairly typical of the pleasant ways a family did things together, but more often it was probably a "nutting" party.

This is still a good idea, and it can be a lot of fun. Pack a picnic, take along some brown bags to hold the "pickings," pile the kids in the family wagon, and go on safari to round up a supply of black walnuts. They're easy to find along the sides of country roads, and they have a number of uses. After the nuts are gathered, spread them out to dry on the ground until the hulls turn black and can be removed easily.

The juice of walnut shells makes a marvelous vegetable dye for fabric or yarn and an excellent stain for leather or wood. Depending on the strength, it will give a color anywhere from amber to almost black. To make the stain, mash rotted hulls, cover with hot water, allow to steep, and then strain. If it isn't going to be used at once, add a little sodium benzoate as a preservative.

When the hulls have been removed, the nuts should be hung in bags to dry and ripen. Then comes the cracking. For this we have always used an old flatiron and hammer. (This is a good, leisurely, sitting-down activity.) You put the iron upside down, bracing the handle between your knees, which gives you a flat surface on which to do the cracking. Turn a nut on its narrow edge (don't hold it on the flat side where a line indicates it *should* open), hold it firmly against the flatiron, give it a sharp tap with the hammer, and try to avoid hitting your thumb. This works with all nuts that have hard shells and usually results in getting two perfect halves, but even if some get crushed or broken, no matter; they'll taste just as good.

Another interesting by-product of walnuts is "buttons," which are especially attractive for use on sweaters or tweed jackets. To make the buttons, put a walnut in a vise to hold it firmly; then saw it into even slices about ⅛ inch thick. Remove bits of nutmeat, sand both sides until smooth, rub in a little walnut stain, and wax.

If you take the easy way out and just purchase shelled black walnuts, you'll miss out on the fun and the interesting by-products, but you'll still have the makings of some of the best of all nut dishes. Chocolate fudge, divinity, and nut bread can be made with any kind of nuts, but they're all better with black walnuts.

For a NUT BREAD that is easy to make and mighty good to eat, sift together 2 C unbleached white flour, ½ C sugar, 2 tsp baking powder, and 1 tsp salt. Add 1 egg yolk, 1 C milk, and ¾ C coarsely chopped black walnuts. Stir and beat until well mixed, turn into greased 5-by-9-inch loaf pan, let stand 20 minutes, and then bake about 45 minutes at 350°.

Black walnuts and prunes are also good go-togethers, especially when they're combined in a moist SPICY PRUNE CAKE. At high speed mix 1 C each sugar and soft butter. When light and fluffy, beat in 2 whole eggs. When smooth, turn down speed and add 1 C prune pulp. Continuing to beat slowly, add ½ C sour cream alternately with 1½ C cake flour sifted with 1½ tsp soda, 1 tsp cinnamon, ¾ tsp cloves, and ½ tsp salt. When batter is smooth, add 1 C coarsely broken or chopped black walnuts. Pour into 9-inch tube pan that has been buttered and floured and bake at 350° for about 1 hour. This is good with a vanilla-flavored seven-minute icing, or even better with a thin butter frosting flavored with the grated rind and juice of 1 lemon.

One member of the hickory family, the pecan, is available everywhere, the year round, but I buy them in quantity around Thanksgiving, put them up in plastic bags that hold about a cup each, and store them in the freezer. This keeps them fresh and ready to use, year round. (Incidentally, this also makes it more difficult for the Pecan Thieves to find the supply!)

One of our favorite pecan goodies is so rich I call it EL FATSO PECAN PIE. It couldn't be easier to make, but oh, that calorie count! In a saucepan combine 1 C sugar with 1½ C corn syrup, heat to boil, and cook about 3 minutes; then pour slowly over 4 beaten eggs, beating constantly until mixture is well blended. Add 4 T butter, 1 tsp vanilla, and 1½ C broken pecans. Pour into unbaked pie crust and bake 45 minutes at 350°. Then, since you might as well be hung for a sheep as a lamb, serve it topped with whipped cream!

For less lavish portions—in fact, bite-size tarts that make excellent party fare—use the same filling in little cocktail-size croutelettes. They come ready to fill and bake, about 30 to a package, and each will hold about 1 teaspoon of filling. Bake at slightly lower heat for less time and serve with just a dab of whipped cream

Many fruitcakes call for the combination of fruits and pecans, but here is one with a difference, called BISHOP'S CAKE. The addition of chocolate gives it that extra something. At high speed mix 3 eggs with 1 C sugar until thick and smooth. Turn speed down and blend in 1 C each chopped dates and halved candied cherries, 2 C broken pecans, and 4 ounces chocolate bits. When well mixed blend in 1½ C all-purpose flour that has been sifted with 1½ tsp soda and ¼ tsp salt. When well mixed, turn batter into greased and floured 5-by-9-inch loaf pan and bake about 90 minutes at 325°. When done, brush with brandy, wrap in foil, and store in refrigerator. To serve, cut into very thin slices.

Hickory, pecan, black walnut, butternut, and hazelnut trees all do well in this climate. They are handsome for landscape use and not only provide shade and beauty but good crops of nuts. Many of them take years to come to full maturity but may start bearing as early as a year or two after transplanting. The important thing is to buy stock of varieties that have been selected for size, flavor, and productivity. If you already have established nut trees growing on your place, it is not only possible but very easy to graft scions of more desirable selections on them.

Many reliable nurseries offer a limited selection of nut trees, but the New York State Fruit Testing Cooperative, Geneva, New York 14456, is an excellent source for many varieties of nuts, in addition to many fine old varieties of fruits not available elsewhere. Whether your nut crop comes from your own trees, roadside bounty, or the supermarket shelf—in shell or out—now is the time to get cracking and start cooking with some of these great American natives.

Corn, the All-American Grain

The Indians they digg many holes . . . and put into thes holes 4 or 5 curnels of ther wheat [corn].
—*Capt. John Smith, 1600*

IN almost 200 years we have not succeeded in selecting a national flower, although a number of different ones have been proposed. Isn't it about time to give credit where it is due, recognize the significance and symbolism of the corn tassel—and make it our official national flower? Is there any other single native plant that is so closely linked to our history, traditions, customs, and economy—or that can be utilized in so many ways?

Corn was a mainstay of the Indian diet; it literally saved many early settlers from death by starvation; and, in certain regions, generations of Americans have been raised on corn bread, greens, fatback, and pot likker. (This may sound like a deprivation diet, but as a matter of fact the combination of nutritional elements is more well rounded than the sugar-flake empty-calorie foods consumed today.)

In 1607 Captain John Smith wrote of the Indians,

"Their corne they rost in the eare green . . . and bruising it in a mortar, lappe it in rowles in the leaves [husks] and so boyle it for a daintie." He told how they dried corn "and in winter they esteeme it being boyled with beans for a rare dish." He described how they ground it into "flower," sifted it through a basket, mixed the resulting meal with water, and formed it into cakes, "Couering them with ashes until they be baked . . . or else boyle them in water and eating the broth with the bread," saving the "coarse grouts and peeces remaining and boiling until tender."

Hominy, samp, succotash (even the names came from the Indians), grits, cakes (ash-, hoe-, and johnny-), dodgers, mush, and tamales came down in a straight line. Indian pudding, spoon bread, muffins, crisps, puffs, hush puppies, and countless other good dishes we enjoy today are just variations on the earliest uses.

Maize, as it is called in Europe, was probably introduced to Spain before 1500 by Columbus. Two and a half centuries later it was still considered a curiosity, not readily available in many places. In 1741 Peter Collinson, in London, wrote John Custis, in Williamsburg, "There is a species of Indian Corn or Maize that Ripens sooner than the Great common Maize, it is called Rair Ripe . . . this is fittest for Our Cultivation where our summer is short. If such grows with you pray send Mee 2 or 3 Ears."

It must have been sent and planted, for in 1743 another letter from Collinson says, "I thank you for the Rare Ripe Corn. . . . I have had 2 most Excellent puddens made of the Flower, How my Wife manages it I can't tell but it is one of the best of puddens."

In Jefferson's garden book there are numerous references to corn, several varieties he experimented with at Shadwell and Monticello. In a letter from Paris in 1787, during the time he was serving as Minister to France, he wrote Nicholas Lewis, his manager in Albemarle:

> I cultivate in my garden here Indian corn for the use of my own table to eat green in our manner, but the

species I am able to get here for seed, is hard with a thick skin, & dry. I had at Monticello a species of small white rare ripe corn which we call Homonycorn, and of which we used to make about 20 barrels a year for table use, green, in homony, & in bread. . . . I wish it were possible for me to receive an ear of this in time for next year . . . more at your leisure I would ask you to send me also an ear or two of the drying corn from the Cherokee country.

One of the easiest ways to cook the corn "flower" is to make CORNMEAL MUSH. Mother used to just sprinkle the dry meal into boiling water with one hand, stirring constantly with the other. She had the knack for doing this and knowing when it was just right. A lot of people don't, but not to worry. Just mix 2 C cornmeal with 2 C cold water and 2 tsp salt; stir this paste into 6 C boiling water, lower heat, and stir constantly until mush starts to thicken; then cover and cook over very low heat for about 20 minutes, stirring occasionally. We used to have mush regularly for Sunday night supper, ladled into soup plates, topped with lumps of butter, brown sugar, and cream or rich milk, and served with crisp buttered toast.

Any left over was poured into a bread pan which had been rinsed with cold water and chilled overnight, for a breakfast the next morning of FRIED MUSH. Turn out the molded mush, slice fairly thin, dredge lightly with flour, and fry on each side until golden and crusty. Serve with butter and syrup.

Another good way to start the day is with batty cakes for breakfast—a Derby Day tradition in Kentucky and an everyday event throughout the South. I still have happy memories of the times I might go by the Alexanders before they had finished breakfast. There was always the same scene around the old gateleg table in the kitchen: the Judge and Miss Cora tucking in batty cakes, Azeele presiding at the electric grill while eating her share, and the resident dog and cat at the back door, waiting their turn. I never had to be asked twice to "take down a plate and pull up a chair." We don't have them on such a regular basis because I don't have a sit-down grill and have to stand at the stove and cook them on an old seasoned griddle. But about two days a week we do start the day the right way.

For BATTY CAKES for the two of us and some extras for Chaka, I sift together ½ C cornmeal, ¼ tsp soda, and 1 tsp salt and stir in an egg and enough buttermilk to make a thin batter. When smooth, stir in about 3 T bacon grease. Drop by tablespoon on hot griddle and brown on both sides. These are very thin and tender, delicious with butter and syrup, or served with a savory hash. I even sneak out an occasional one and eat it just with butter, while waiting for everyone else to get filled.

Gene and Joe Prendergast, who live at Oak Hill (the former home of President Monroe), are a shining example of the way to treat our native corn and its by-products with proper respect. Out in the fields Joe raises the white corn which goes to the mill to be ground. Gene plans the most interesting meals, which more often than not include some type of corn bread—whether packed in picnic baskets for guests to take out to some inviting spot in the large garden or formally served at the banquet table in the dining room. Down in the old kitchen, in an ancient stove, Ida turns out these delectable breads, muffins, sticks, and a procession of other good things made from cornmeal.

For OAK HILL CORN BREAD sift together ½ C each cornmeal and flour, 2 tsp baking powder, and 1 tsp each sugar and salt. Stir in 1 egg beaten with 1 C sweet milk and 2 T corn oil. Pour into well-buttered pan, 8 by 8 by 2 inches, and bake at 350° until golden brown. This recipe also makes good muffins, baked at 375° until golden brown (time required depends on size of muffin pans).

SKILLET CORN BREAD is the type I always bake when we are making a meal of everything from the garden: cooked snaps, new potatoes, and corn; fresh tomatoes, onions, and cucumbers. Sift together 2 C cornmeal, 1 tsp salt, and ½ tsp soda. Mix in 1 egg and enough buttermilk to make a fairly thick batter. Heat 4 T bacon drippings in an iron skillet, turn skillet to coat sides and bottom, pour balance into batter, give it a stir or two, and turn it out into the hot skillet. Bake at 375° until crusty and brown. Any left over is split and toasted under the broiler and then served with creamed dried beef or some kind of hash.

For everyday SPOON BREAD, which we have often, pour 1 C boiling water over 1 C cornmeal. Add 1 tsp salt and ¼ C butter and mix until smooth. When cool, stir in 1 tsp baking powder and 3 egg yolks that have been beaten with 2 C sweet milk. When well blended fold in the stiffly beaten whites of the 3 eggs, pour into well-buttered soufflé dish, and bake 30 to 40 minutes at 375°. For special occasions I make Sarah's Spoon Bread (page 173).

CORN PONE, dodgers, ash-, hoe-, or johnnycakes—all are made about the same. Lacking the ashes or a hoe, bake them in the oven. Mix 2 C cornmeal with 1 tsp salt and 1 T bacon drippings. Add enough water to make a stiff dough, pat into pones or cakes, leaving the imprint of four fingers across the top, and bake on a greased tin at 375° until golden brown.

More delicate little patties are CORN CRISPS, delicious served with a salad luncheon. To 1 C cornmeal and 1 tsp salt, add ¾ C boiling water. Stir until smooth and let cool. Then fold in the stiffly beaten whites of 4 eggs, drop by teaspoon on hot buttered baking sheets, and bake at 400° until light golden color.

Grits—singular or plural? One young guest solved her dilemma with the comment, "This grits sure are good." I don't know how the term "a set of grits" originated, just where: the South. The Indian corn "flower" was similar to our meal. The "grouts and peeces" were comparable to grits. Regular grits is ground from the inner white corn. Yellow grits is ground from the husk of the grain. Big hominy is the whole dried grain with the husk removed by threshing. For samp or lye hominy, the dried whole grains of corn are soaked in lye to remove the husk, dried again, and then brought back to a puffed state by boiling and soaking in cold water. Samp or lye hominy is what we buy in cans, ready to heat and serve.

Now, back to that "SET OF GRITS." To 5 C cold water add 1 C grits and 1 tsp salt. Bring to boil and cook slowly, stirring occasionally, until done—about 30 minutes. Serve hot, with butter or RED-EYE GRAVY, made by adding some water and a little bit of coffee to a skillet in which a slice of country ham has been fried.

There are a lot of interesting things to do with leftover cooked grits: chill, slice, and fry like mush; or brush thin slices with melted butter, sprinkle with cheese and paprika, and bake in a hot oven until the cheese bubbles. Two cups of leftover grits is enough to make CHEESE GRITS SOUFFLÉ. To 2 C cooked grits add 2 C hot milk and stir until mixture is smooth. When cool, add 1 tsp baking powder, the beaten yolks of 2 eggs, and 2 C shredded cheese. Mix, then fold in the stiffly beaten whites of the 2 eggs, pour into buttered baking dish, and bake at 375° until puffed and golden in color.

From corn, of course, we get bourbon, and among other useful and stimulating purposes it serves, it makes a BOURBON SAUCE that will transform something as mundane as bread pudding. Mix 1 C sugar with 3 T water and stir over heat until dissolved. Stir in ½ C butter and, when it is melted, quickly stir in 1 beaten egg. Continuing to stir, cook over low heat until smooth and slightly thickened. Remove from heat and add ⅓ C bourbon.

Less familiar is CORN COB SYRUP, which is different in flavor but every bit as good as maple syrup. To 2 gallons of water add 12 red corncobs that have been broken into short lengths. Boil uncovered until liquid is reduced by half. Strain. Return liquid to kettle with 2 pounds of granulated and 1 pound of brown sugar. Stir until dissolved and cook until desired consistency is reached. Pour into sterilized jars or bottles and seal. Serve in all the usual ways —with pancakes, waffles, etc.—but save some for a sauce, poured over vanilla ice cream.

Corncobs also make good pipes, for smoking tobacco

or blowing bubbles. Grind them for an excellent garden mulch or an additive to cattle feed.

Charming little dolls can be made from the corn husks or shucks, which are also used for tamale wrappers and making various "fake" flowers for unusual arrangements. They can also be woven into rugs or mats; braided for hats, handbags, and baskets; made into hearth brooms and mops; and used to make birdhouses, hanging baskets for plants, or covers for flowerpots.

We haven't even considered the many ways in which fresh, or green, corn is used. Most of them are familiar to everyone. But let's not forget the stalks. When fresh they have a sweet sap, similar to sorghum—good for chewing. Selected stalks and tassels are effective additions to dried arrangements. And finally, the dried stalks can go back to enrich the land for future crops; you can chop them from small areas to add to the compost heap, or they can come from the combine right onto the field, ready to be disked back into the ground to provide humus and nutrients for *more corn.*

Do I hear a motion to make the corn tassel our national flower?

Thanksgiving Feast Coming Up

Great as the preparations were for the dinner, everything was so contrived that not a soul in the house should be kept from the morning service of Thanksgiving.
—Harriet Beecher Stowe, Oldtown Folks

WHETHER some of the members celebrate the day by attending church, watching parades and football games, or heading out to the fields to hunt (fox or bird), Thanksgiving remains essentially a family day, and the more the big feast can be "contrived" ahead of time, the more pleasant the whole day is for everyone, especially the cook.

Not that any of us tries to put on a production comparable to the times of which Mrs. Stowe was writing. Just to read an old menu is enough to make me tired and take my appetite. It sounds more like an endurance contest than a celebration.

Today's Thanksgiving dinner may seem almost austere by comparison, but the basics probably remain about the same even though the menu may vary, depending on regional differences, family traditions, and changing tastes. Certainly most of us will settle for less variety and fewer courses, but even so, with limitations of time and energy, plus little or no help with the "contriving," we need to do some advance planning and preparation.

With a week to go there are a number of things that can and should be done to avoid a last-minute hassle or ending up in a state of decline.

If you select a frozen turkey, get it ahead of time and store in your home freezer or make arrangements to pick it up just in time to start thawing. This way you'll be sure of getting the size and type you want. When possible, I prefer a fresh turkey.

ROAST TURKEY. The way I cook turkey depends on the size of the bird and my own schedule during the cooking time. Preparing it for either method is the same. First, remove all excess fat, to be rendered separately and used in various dishes later on. Cook neck and giblets separately, in water, to make broth. After the dressed bird has been rinsed and patted dry, lightly salt the cavity, then put in a whole onion, some celery leaves and sprigs of fresh rosemary, a small red pepper, and either an apple or some strips of lemon or orange peel. This replaces the more usual stuffing, which I cook separately.

Rub the outside surface of the bird with lemon juice, instead of butter or oil, and sprinkle lightly with coarse salt, flour, freshly ground pepper, and paprika. If the bird is small, around 10 pounds, and I'm going to be available for "basting," I just put it in an open roasting pan, add a little water, and roast it at 300° for about 20 minutes per pound, basting from time to time with pan juices (and adding some of the cooked broth if necessary). When bird is brown, cover lightly with foil and continue cooking until done.

If the bird is larger or I'm going to be busy doing other things during the cooking time, I put the prepared turkey in a paper bag, fold over the end and staple it or seal it with tape, place it on the rack of large broiler pan, put it in a 300° oven, and forget about it until it is done. A 10-to-15-pound bird will take 20 minutes per pound, 15-to-18-pounders, 18 minutes, 18-to-20-pounders, 15 minutes, 20-to-23-pounders, 13 minutes. At end of required cooking time, remove from oven, let stand a few minutes, puncture bottom of bag to let juices run down into pan, and lift out the bird to "settle" for about 20 minutes before carving.

There will probably be more rich juice than you'll need for gravy; it is really too rich to be used as is and should be combined with some of the broth made from the giblets. Any not needed for gravy should be stored in the refrigerator for use in hash, soup, or other follow-up turkey dishes.

TURKEY STUFFING, or dressing, starts with making Skillet Corn Bread (page 186). When cool, this corn bread is crumbled and added to an equal amount of regular bread or biscuits broken into large crumbs. Add 2 or 3 chopped onions and ribs of celery that have been wilted in butter and season with salt, pepper, sage, and parsley.

Melt ½ C butter in 1 C hot water or broth, add to crumb mixture, and toss lightly. If mixture requires more moisture, add hot water. With ice cream scoop lift out balls of dressing, place in buttered muffin tins or space on baking sheet, and top each one with a bit of butter. Bake at 350° until crusty and done.

These dressing balls can be made several days ahead of time, stored in the freezer, and reheated at the last minute before serving. The same basic dressing mixture can be used to make a great OYSTER CASSEROLE. In a baking dish place a layer of uncooked stuffing, cover with a layer of oysters, and repeat layers, ending with topping of the stuffing. Pour oyster liquor over, dot with butter, and bake at 350° until light brown and done.

Creamed onions are a favorite but such a chore when you have to peel the small whole onions and cook them just to the right stage without falling apart. One thing for which I am truly thankful is that tiny, whole, frozen onions can now be gotten by the bag. A few days ahead you can make a light cream sauce, add the frozen onions, bake, and then refreeze or refrigerate to be heated again shortly before serving.

As for starches, I'm always of two minds about mashed potatoes. While I could easily eat my weight in them I loathe having to peel, cook, and prepare them when there are so many other things already on the fire. Grits, brown rice, or bulgur are a heap easier and almost as good. As for sweet potatoes or squash, with pumpkin pie coming up who needs them? For that matter, who needs hot rolls? Well, nobody—but everyone feels cheated without them. Fortunately they can be made, baked, and frozen well ahead of time and reheated at the last minute.

Vegetables vary from year to year. One year a handsome crop of purple cauliflower was an obvious choice. This year the groundhogs pruned the plants back so many times there were still no flower heads by killing frost. There are other garden substitutes in the freezer, but I'll probably settle for SMOTHERED CARROTS, they're so good and so easy. In a large skillet melt about ½ stick butter, add a layer of thinly sliced onions, and then small whole carrots or larger ones quartered. Add salt and pepper but *no* water or other liquid. Cover and cook on *very low* heat until carrots are done.

The salad is unchanging from year to year: aspic made with home-done tomato juice with herbs, served on a bed of curly endive or fresh watercress. Instead of the usual celery there will be slices of fennel bulb, which did do well this year, paper-thin slices of Jerusalem artichoke marinated in French dressing, and ripe olives. Of course there will be cranberry sauce and Watermelon Pickle (page 135), and if anyone still has space for it, the grand finale is pumpkin pie.

This particular PUMPKIN PIE is so good it shouldn't have to share the spotlight with any other kind of pie or cake or pudding. The difference between this and other versions is that the pumpkin pulp is cooked down until the natural sugars have sort of caramelized. In a large heavy skillet slowly cook down 1 large and 1 small can of pumpkin over very low heat (stirring often) until it is thick and has darkened considerably in color. Place this hot pumpkin in a large bowl and add 1 C each of light brown and white sugar, 2 T molasses, 3 tsp each ground cinnamon and ginger, 1 tsp salt, and ¼ tsp cloves. Stir until sugar is dissolved and spices are well mixed in. Add 4 large eggs that have been slightly beaten and stir until smooth. Finally, blend in 3 C scalded milk. Turn into two 9-inch pans lined with unbaked crust. Bake at 450° for ten minutes; lower heat to 350° and bake 30 minutes longer. Space pecan halves on surface of pies, return to heat, and bake another 10 minutes. Serve with sweetened whipped cream that has been flavored with vanilla.

This represents a lot of effort for one meal but the combination of everything is mighty good, and if I make extra amounts while I'm at it, I can sort of coast on cooking for the next two or three days.

Of course, if you aren't strong on tradition you can skip all this. Go out for Thanksgiving dinner, broil a steak, boil up a pot of beans, or pick up a cheeseburger to eat on the run. But you'll be missing a lot.

DECEMBER
Cookie Time–Christmas Is a Comin'

These cookies are pretty to hang upon the tree during Christmas week, and to pass in baskets to holiday callers.

—*From an old cookbook*

WHETHER you have a Cookie Monster in the house, want to bake and decorate a batch of ginger boys, girls, angels, and critters for the Christmas tree, or would just like to have a supply of goodies that can be made ahead of time and set aside for serving during the holidays or giving as gifts, now is the time to get started on a cookie-baking caper.

Some types must be made and stored well ahead of time to "ripen" before they're ready to eat. A few are fairly tedious and time-consuming to make, but so good they're well worth setting aside a special day when they can be concentrated on without distractions and interruptions. Still others are so easy that the youngest cooks can put them together and even tiny tots can roll them into balls for baking.

Cookies may vary considerably in name, size, shape,

flavor, and texture, but there is scarcely a country or culture in which some type of these little sweet cakes is not associated with festive occasions and traditionally served with some beverage—tea, coffee, milk, hot chocolate, wine, eggnog, or punch.

Each year I add a few shapes to my collection of cutters, the most recent set being for engine and cars that should delight children or amuse those grown-up children, model railroad buffs. And after years spent messing around with knives, light finally dawned and I found that cutting wheels (both the straight-edge types used for pizza and the fluted types intended for pie crust) are just the thing for cutting diamond shapes, diagonals, strips, and squares.

In assembling supplies don't forget to add a can of nonstick spray to go on all cutting tools (scissors, knives, wheels) and shaped cutters. This not only makes it easier to chop all the sticky things like candied fruits or figs and dates, but it also enables you to work with somewhat softer dough mixes that otherwise stick to a knife or cutter. And be sure to get a cake of beeswax (the kind sewing shops sell for waxing thread) to rub over hot baking sheets to prevent cookies from sticking; it's much more effective than the usual greasing and adds a lovely aroma to the other good smells coming from the oven.

If you plan to decorate cookies, invest in one or two pans for making tiny muffins or cupcakes; they make all-purpose containers for several icing colors or for an assortment of silver shot, "hundreds and thousands," cocoa, red-hots, chocolate sprinkles, or things you may want to dip cookies into before baking. Don't forget to have a few cheap paintbrushes for applying glazes, icings, or colors and an assortment of small bottles of food coloring. A lemon peeler run over the surface of stiff dough will make even, tiny, round strips for raised decorations. The garlic press is great for making "hair," including beards and sideburns, or "feathers" for angel wings; just force some stiff dough through the press onto cookies before baking.

Springerle molds or rolling pins are nice to have for

pressing raised designs, but, failing these, take a look around at what you have that could be used for the same purpose: salt dishes, shakers, glasses, or vases may all have a molded shape in the base that can be used. For making small circles of various sizes there are thimbles, the little metal or plastic cases that some film comes in, pill bottles, and various tin cans (tomato paste, frozen juice, liver paté, and mushrooms give a good assortment of sizes).

There are, of course, many tinned foods that come in cans that will make larger circles, and anchovies, kippers, and sardines will provide oval, oblong, or square cutters. After the tin has been emptied, just remove the bottom, smooth down edges on both ends with a pair of pliers, if necessary, and *voila!* more cutters for your collection. You can use a paper pattern of any shape and just cut around it with the cutting wheel, or turn the kids loose and let them cut free forms of any shape that suits their fancy and decorate them with equal abandon.

GREAT AUNT JANE'S GINGER COOKIES. Now for the basic dough. (Even if you have to rely on a wooden spoon and a strong right arm it isn't difficult to put together, but if you have a mixer with a dough hook, all the easier.) In large mixer bowl whip 1½ C heavy cream until stiff. Add 2½ C dark brown sugar, 1¼ C dark corn syrup, 1 T each powdered ginger and grated lemon rind, and 2 T baking soda and stir until well blended and smooth. Change beater to dough hook and on moderate speed start adding flour, about ½ C at a time. It will take about 9 C of flour in all to make the required stiff dough. When mixed, place the dough in a plastic bag, covered plastic container, or bowl and store it in the refrigerator or another cool place. It must be left for a day or two and it can be stored for more than a week, which is a help if you don't want to bake the entire batch at one go.

When ready to bake, take an easily handled portion of dough and roll thin on a lightly floured board or marble slab. Cut out shapes, lift with pancake turner, and slip onto waxed baking sheet. Brush surface of cookies with water and bake about 15 minutes in a 250° oven. When done, slide from pan onto flat surface covered with wax paper. Bake all cookie shapes before starting to decorate (they can be stored in a covered container until you're ready to decorate them).

For BASIC ICING, mix 1 slightly beaten egg white with 1 C powdered sugar. When smooth, divide into portions to be colored different tints and shades. Add coloring drop by drop until you get the desired shade. Leave a good portion of the icing white, to be used as is or covered with a colored glaze. To make glazed colors, add a small amount of water and color to a small portion of egg yolk (one yolk will make a lot of glaze). I make both icing and glaze thin enough to spread with paintbrushes of different sizes, thinning with brandy, rose water, or kirsch.

If you have any helpers too young to be unleashed on rolling and cutting operations, give them the job of making little BROWN PEPPERNUTS, more fun than play clay and as easy as making mud pies. In a large saucepan put 1 C each of lard, dark brown sugar, and molasses and bring to boil. Remove from heat and pour into large bowl of mixer, adding 1 tsp each of soda, salt, ginger, cloves, and allspice and ½ tsp freshly ground black pepper. Mix until blended. Replace beater with dough hook and at moderate speed continue mixing, while adding enough flour to make a stiff dough. Store in a cool place for a day or two.

If young helpers are making the "nuts," give them their own working space. The bottom side of a square of oilcloth, when lightly floured, makes an excellent surface for rolling out cookies, and it can be placed on any tabletop or counter. Spoon out dough in portions; 1 teaspoonful is about right. Each portion of dough should be rolled around on the "board," using the palm of one hand, until it makes a smooth ball. Space the balls about 1 inch apart on waxed baking sheet and bake until brown, about 15 minutes at 325°.

These "nuts" do not spread in baking and they should

be made small, for they're not for biting or chewing but meant to be popped in the mouth to melt on the tongue and be savored slowly. The ideal way to consume them is to sit in a comfortable chair by an open fire, reading a good book with a bowl of Brown Peppernuts and a crisp, juicy apple by your side. You can slowly work your way through a powerful number of these spicy little "nuts" in an evening, and I do declare the calming effect beats transcendental meditation.

Now WHITE PEPPERNUTS are suited to more convivial occasions, spent in the company of others. In the large mixer bowl, at high speed, beat together 5 eggs with 2 C granulated sugar until very light and fluffy. Add grated rind of 1 lemon, 1 T cinnamon, 1 tsp freshly grated nutmeg, ½ tsp each ground cloves and white pepper, and 2 tsp baking powder. At moderate speed, mix until thoroughly blended. Mix in 3 ounces thinly slivered citron and 4 C flour (unsifted). Chill dough overnight, roll into balls a bit more than 1 inch in size, space on baking sheet to allow for spreading, and bake at 350° until very light golden color. While they are warm from the oven, drop them in a large brown bag with about 1 C powdered sugar, shake to coat cakes with sugar, and then shift to wax-paper-covered surface to cool before storing.

If you want to make an awe-inspiring supply of excellent little cookies, proceed with this traditional recipe for MORAVIAN CHRISTMAS CAKES. They need a week or two to "ripen," and after that they keep for ages. One year I made them a bit late and they weren't ready for Christmas, so I set them aside and forgot about them. A couple of months later a gaggle of small boys came down for the day and I remembered the Moravian cookies, a 25-pound lard can filled with them. You should have seen those eyes bug out when I brought out this can of cookies and gave the kids *carte blanche*. Later, one of their mothers said, "I hear that John's mama has the biggest cookie jar in the world."

If you would go and do likewise, heat 1 quart of

molasses and pour over ¾ C each of lard and butter. Stir until mixed. Add 1½ C light brown sugar, 4 T brandy, 1 T mace, 2 T each of ground cloves and cinnamon, the grated rind of 1 lemon, and 2 T baking soda. Add all-purpose flour to make a stiff dough (it will take 12 to 15 C). Store in a cool place overnight and next day, or on a succession of days, roll out very thin on a lightly floured board and cut into stars or crescents or rounds. Bake in 375° oven. After cooling, store in tins to ripen.

GREAT AUNT JANE'S OAT CRISPS have to be the best oatmeal cookies you ever ate, and they're very easy to make. Sift together 2½ C of sifted flour and 1 tsp each of soda and salt. Add and mix thoroughly 1 C brown sugar, 1 C shortening, and ½ C water. Add 2½ C regular rolled oats. Mix, roll out thin (using powdered sugar instead of flour on the board), cut into rounds, and bake at 350°.

SUPER CHOCOLATE COOKIES. Here's another where the children can do the "rolling." Melt 2 squares bitter chocolate, add ½ C shortening, 1⅔ C granulated sugar, and 2 tsp vanilla, and beat with 2 beaten eggs until smooth. Sift together 2 C flour, 2 tsp baking powder, and ½ tsp salt. Add to first mixture alternately with ⅓ C milk. Chill until dough is stiff. Shape with hands into small balls, roll in granulated sugar, space on sheet to allow spreading, and bake 20 minutes at 350°.

I'm not a great one for sweets, but I could easily eat my weight in SAND BARS, these little cousins of Scotch shortbread. Cream together ½ C butter and 2 T granulated sugar. Then, with hands, work in 2 C flour and 1 C finely chopped pecans. Form into little finger rolls and bake 15 minutes in 325° oven; then, while hot, roll in powdered sugar.

From Sweden comes a distinctive butter cookie, called DREAMS. In saucepan melt and slightly brown 1 C sweet fresh butter and pour into bowl of mixer. When lukewarm, add ¾ C sugar and 2 tsp vanilla and beat at high speed until the mixture is fluffy. Turn down speed and slowly blend 2 C flour sifted with 1 tsp baking powder. When smooth, chill dough for 1 hour or so. With hands, roll out into small balls, space about 2 inches apart on prepared baking sheet, press half a blanched almond in top of each, and bake at 250° until light golden color (about 30 minutes).

Thin "crisps," or rolled wafers, are typical of many regions or countries. All of them are good; here are two that are different and not too temperamental. (Good results will be more predictable, however, if they're made when the weather is not damp and humid.)

SOUTHERN CRISPS. At high speed beat ⅜ C butter with ¾ C sugar until light and fluffy. Add 1 egg and continue beating at high speed for 2 minutes. Reduce speed of mixer and blend in ¾ C unsifted flour, ¾ C finely ground pecans, and 1 T vanilla. When mixture is smooth, drop by half teaspoonfuls on prepared baking sheets, about 3 inches apart. Smooth down each portion with back of spoon that has been dipped in ice water. Bake at 400° about 6 minutes. With wide spatula or pancake turner, loosen cookies quickly as soon as removed from oven; otherwise cookies will be too crisp to remove from pan. Store in airtight containers. (Batter may be stored in refrigerator indefinitely before baking.)

ROLLED WAFERS can be formed a number of different ways. Perhaps the easiest is to cover a broomstick with aluminum foil and prop it on the backs of a couple of chairs. This gives you enough space to work fast, which is essential. In a skillet combine ½ C each butter and sugar, ⅔ C ground almonds, 1 T flour, and 2 T milk. Stir and heat until butter melts. Drop by teaspoon on greased and floured baking sheet, about 4 inches apart. Bake at 350° until light brown, about 8 minutes. Working quickly, lift each cookie and lay over broom handle, rolling pin, or wooden spoon handle to shape. When cold, store with wax paper between layers, in tightly covered container.

DELICATE LEMON WAFERS can be baked any old time, and they can be turned out in nothing flat—or almost! In mixer bowl combine ½ C sugar with ½ C soft butter. Blend at high speed until fluffy, add 2 eggs, and continue mixing at high speed until smooth. Lower speed and blend in 1 C flour and the grated rind of 1 lemon. Drop by teaspoon on prepared baking sheet, about 2 inches apart, and bake at 350° about 7 minutes, or until edges are lightly browned. These are thin, crisp, and a "must" to serve with eggnog in some parts of the South.

For MERINGUE KISSES, combine 2 egg whites with a pinch of salt in large bowl of mixer. Beat at high speed until stiff, turn down speed a bit, and continue beating while adding, slowly, 1 C sugar. Finally add flavoring: ½ tsp each vanilla and lemon rind or 1 tsp of any liqueur or other flavoring. With teaspoon drop batter on lightly greased baking sheet, lifting spoon from center to make a sort of point on top of each kiss. Bake at 250° about 20 minutes. Remove from pans while hot.

To vary this recipe, after flavoring has been added fold in 1 C finely chopped or ground nuts (filberts, black walnuts, and pecans are all good) or a combination of ½ C each of ground nuts and finely minced candied fruit.

While batches of cookie dough are chilling or "resting" before being baked, take out enough time to make LEMON JELLIED APPLES. They're wonderful to have on hand and would make a grand gift. Simple and easy, this amount will make at least 12 servings. They're good with sliced cold meats, especially pork roast, ham, or turkey, can be served for dessert with a glob of sour cream, and even make a great sweet to slice and serve on bread or toast, for tea or breakfast.

In a large shallow pan (I use a large, heavy skillet with a tight-fitting lid) combine 1 C sugar, 2 C water, and the thinly shredded rind and juice of 1 lemon. Cook and stir on medium heat until sugar is dissolved; then add 6 large firm apples (Yorks are good for this) which have been pared, cored, and quartered. As each apple is prepared, drop and turn in syrup to prevent darkening. When all are done, cover pan, bring contents to a simmer, and cook until apples are cooked through (test for doneness with broomstraw or fork tines). With a slotted spoon lift out apples and transfer them to a dish or bowl that can be covered. Increase heat and continue cooking syrup until it begins to thicken; then pour over apples, cover, and chill. This should be made at least a day before using, but if kept chilled and covered it will keep for 2 or 3 weeks.

After the cookie jars are filled there should still be time to turn out other good things we like to have on hand for the holidays. You can find a lot of recipes for popcorn balls, but I have never seen one for this SUGARED POPCORN Grandmother Nina used to make (and I continue the tradition). Pop a large batch of popcorn but do *not* use any sort of oil or shortening. When corn is all popped, in a large preserving kettle cook 1 C granulated sugar and 1 C water (stirring constantly) for about 5 minutes, dump in popcorn, and toss with a large wooden spoon until corn kernels are coated with the sugary mixture.

WHITE PRALINES are my favorite candy. Over moderately high heat, stir together 3 C granulated sugar and 1 C cream until dissolved. Continue to cook and stir for 15 minutes. Remove from heat and add 1 tsp vanilla and 1 pound pecan meats. Pour onto a greased surface, and, when cool, separate the nut meats.

It has been well over half a century since I sat perched on a kitchen table, watching my father make this DIVINE DIVINITY. In repeated tries, over the years since, my efforts seem to fall short of the superb confection he turned out. But, even so—not bad, not bad at all.

Stir together over low heat 3 C granulated sugar, ¾ C water, and ¾ C white corn syrup. When dissolved, cook over medium heat without stirring, to 290°. Meanwhile, beat until stiff 3 egg whites with a pinch of salt. When syrup is ready, pour very slowly over egg-white mixture, beating constantly. (An electric mixer is almost a must if you haven't a very strong right arm.) When all the syrup is beaten in, add 1 tsp vanilla, ½ C each chopped glazed cherries and pineapple, and 1 C black-walnut meats. Continue beating until mixture loses its gloss; then either drop by spoon onto waxed paper or pour into shallow pan to be cut into squares.

APRICOT CANDY is much less sweet than many other confections and so easy that youngsters can do most of the "making." Put 1 pound dried apricots, 1 whole orange (seedless, or with seeds removed), 1 C shredded coconut and 1 C nutmeats (pecans) through fine blade of grinder. Mix with 1 C white corn syrup and cook in double boiler until mixture is very thick. Cool, roll into small balls, and then, roll either in granulated sugar or ground nuts.

With time running out I find myself wishing I were the type who does Christmas shopping and wrapping in July, instead of waiting until after the last minute and having to mail boxes air express, special delivery, at a cost that exceeds the value of contents. Then I remember that when I have been foresighted and bought gifts out of season they seemed to disappear around wrapping and sending time. Not until Easter did the Christmas cards for the year before come to light! I *could* send them this time around—that is, I could if they hadn't gone back to that big hiding place where the lost things live.

Oh, well, Merry anyhow!

Cups That Cheer

Prepare the song, the feast, the ball,
To welcome merry Christmas.
—William Robert Spencer, "The Joys of Christmas"

THIS is the festive season when our thoughts turn to "bowles" of steaming punch, syllabub, posset, nogs, gloggs, mulled cider, et al. Something with a "stick" in it is traditional for almost everyone at this season of good cheer.

One of our traditions is eggnog, made late on Christmas eve and sampled before going off to bed and sweet drams. It's the real thing (not that travesty prepared by dumping a bottle of booze into some prepared mix), an adaptation of the original Westmorland Club recipe, which starts out with "60 eggs." Next morning we start the day with a mug of nog, sipped while we sit around the open fire and disgorge the contents of the Christmas stockings. Any sort of cup would serve the purpose, I suppose, but it just wouldn't taste the same in anything but our old "God Speed the Plough" mugs.

EGGNOG. In one mixer bowl beat 12 egg whites with a pinch of salt until stiff and set aside. In another bowl, whip 1 pint of heavy cream until stiff and set aside. Remove beater from stand (from here on it is hand-held, for no mixer bowl will hold this quantity) and beat 12 egg yolks that have been put in a large crock or preserving kettle. When yolks are thick and lemony looking, start adding sugar slowly, 1½ C in all, continuing to beat constantly. When batter is thick and smooth start adding brandy or cognac, a little at a time, beating constantly. (It takes a fifth of cognac, and if you add it too fast, at first, it will curdle the egg yolks.) When all the brandy has been added, pour in 1 pint of good dark rum and beat until thoroughly mixed. Turn mixer to low speed and pour in 1 pint of regular cream and 1 quart of whole milk. When all is well blended, remove beater and fold in the stiffly beaten egg whites and cream. To serve, ladle into mugs or cups and dust top with freshly grated nutmeg. In theory it should "ripen" overnight, but nobody ever turns down a sample mug as soon as it is ready.

After making the eggnog there will be enough rum left to make CIDER ICE to serve sometime during the holidays. It is especially good after a heavy meal. To 6 C cider or apple juice add 6 T honey, 4 ounces of rum, and 2 T Grand Marnier. If you're lucky enough to have one of the new ice cream makers, it will do all the work. Otherwise use a regular ice cream freezer or freeze in refrigerator ice trays and take out and beat several times during freezing.

By contrast, CIDER SNOW is one of the easiest drinks to prepare. It contains nothing but fresh sweet cider, tastes delicious, sipped before or throughout dinner, and is particularly good with roast pork. Just fill heavy glasses with fresh cider, put them in the freezer, and leave until the cider is mushy. (I plan to use my recently acquired Picardie goblets, used for wine in all French bistros, but any heavy glass or glass mug will do.)

Cider is like pease porridge; some like it hot. One purist we knew mulled cider or wine by sticking a red-hot poker in the mug of liquid. This obviously calls for a roaring open fire and results in a considerable amount of ashes and soot in your drink. The peculiar flavor can't be duplicated by any other method, and perhaps this is just as well! A more conventional way of making MULLED CIDER is to pour cider in a saucepan, add some whole cloves and stick cinnamon, and heat (do not let it boil). It can be kept hot over a chafing-dish flame or in a fondue pot, and alongside you might have a little jar of honey and a bottle of applejack to be added according to individual taste.

Goops, Christmas KP, and a Chili Roundup

The Goops they lick their fingers,
And the Goops they lick their knives;
They spill their broth on the tablecloth,
Oh, they lead disgusting Lives.
—Gelett Burgess

How many of you remember the Goops? They were cautionary tales for bad children, or generally good children who slipped into bad habits. I can't help but think that they took some of the pressure off parents who otherwise would have had to nag, nag, nag in order to instill some rudiments of polite behavior in the normally savage young. And I can't help wondering if some modern form of cautionary tale would not be a good idea today. I know youth must be served, but do children have to grow up acting as if they came from under a rock or from Lower Slobbovia?

I wouldn't suggest anything as graphic and frightening as the object lessons in "Slovenly Peter," a forerunner of the Goops. Take, for example, Augustus, who would not, would not, eat his soup, he would not eat it, no. Finally he grew thin as a string, and the next day he was dead. The recommended method for stopping thumb-sucking was to cut off the thumb, and the predicted fate for the greedy child was to split in two, right down the middle.

During the forties Munro Leaf wrote a much milder set of maxims, which placed emphasis on minding your p's and q's as well as your manners because the "Watchbird" was "watching you." Now the only influence seems to come from television, which is constant and anything but cautionary. In fact, it seems rather to provide a model for more ways to be impolite and ill-mannered. A lot of people go around behaving as though nobody were "watching you" and what's more wouldn't care if anybody was.

Before and during the holidays I seem to have spent full time home, home on the range (and I don't mean the one where the buffaloes roam) and around the clock on KP duty. One morning, shortly after midnight, I got up to wrestle a ham to the mat, getting it boiled and baked. Several mornings around two, I started steaming puddings or cutting out cookies. The muscle cramps in my legs went well beyond the aid of the horse liniment, and most of the time I felt ready to drop in my tracks.

Being accustomed to cooking for two, it *do* make a difference to have extra, and voracious, appetites around the round table. Then, what with varying schedules of retiring and arising, nearly every meal turns into a movable feast. By the time one shift is eating breakfast an earlier one is ready for lunch. Long after you think you're finished and done with the midday meal a stray comes wandering in, wondering "what's cooking." The only time I could get everyone corraled, seated at the table at the same time, eating the same thing, was at dinner. And, like the recurrent theme in a Bach fugue, there was nonstop nibbling. It sort of reminded me of the days before the young'uns left the nest, when everything edible that wasn't nailed down was usually consumed before its appointed time.

I'm not sure that I have the stamina and strength to operate like this on a prolonged basis anymore; in fact, I'm sure I haven't, but for the short run it was fun. There were no "picky" eaters on the place. All present tucked into everything that was set before them with obvious and expressed enjoyment. Good food, good wine, good talk, and lots of laughter—this is what I think of while I'm preparing the meal and what I remember long after.

As usual we had turkey, we had country ham, but also as usual our old standby was lots of chili con carne. We had it for supper Christmas Eve, and we dipped into the pot again after the tree was trimmed. Several times someone would heat up some chili to go with a turkey or ham sandwich, and one morning I even devoured a bowl of cold leftover chili for breakfast! Don't know that I'd recommend it as a regular thing, but it surely hit the spot when I had been up working for over four hours and suddenly realized, when it came on light, that I was hungry enough to eat the woodwork.

No matter how you make it, and there are a lot of versions, I don't see how any household can make do without a good supply of chili, either stashed away in the freezer or refrigerator or simmering on the stove. Especially during the holidays when everyone is going different places and doing different things at different times, and the only thing you know for sure is that they are going to be hungry when they check in.

Several months ago, when I wrote about one of my versions I had happened to cook that week, a chiliphile took me to task in no uncertain terms. For one thing I had included 1 T molasses, which he considered *lèse majesté*. For another, my version lacked "machismo"—a basic ingredient of *good* chili, according to my critic, and he went on to say that my "concoction" fell miserably below the standards set at Terlingua.

As a result I was more than usually interested in the outcome of this year's annual Terlingua Chili Cook-off. Since the recipes are secret I don't know if any of them included molasses, but I do know that the winner was a Girl Scout troop. So much for machismo!

Chili con carne is an Americanized dish and not the basic staple of diet in Mexico that it is thought to be. Generally the *carne*, or meat, used is beef, though in my files there are versions that call for pork, veal, mutton, venison, or moose, which is chopped any size from fine dice to 1-inch cubes or coarsely ground. The chiles are a combination of mild and hot types, in amounts that vary considerably, as do additional seasonings. Tomatoes—whole, juice, puree, or paste—may or may not be used, and frijoles or beans—black, pinto, kidney, pink, or red—are either cooked with the chili or served on the side.

The only safe generalization to make about chili con carne is that each chiliphile considers himself to be an expert and a purist, and his own particular version of the dish is "the authentic one."

Commercial chili powder is made up of a blend of mild and hot chiles, cumin, oregano, garlic, onion, and other seasonings. Nearly every line of spices includes a chili powder, but most of them just don't have the power and the flavor that they should have. Some serious chili cooks like one, others prefer another, and still others prefer a third. In Mexican markets and some stores that sell Mexican food in this country you can buy powders of the pure chile, ranging from mild and sweet, to pungent, to hot.

Sometimes I use a commercial blend; then again I may grind and mix my own powder blend and sometimes soak the dried chiles to make a liquid sauce. I have a sizable collection of hot peppers that range in intensity from hot to sizzling to permanently impaired taste buds.

Goops, Christmas KP, and a Chili Roundup

These include pico de pajaro, chiltepin, chile pequin, jalapeno, and morita, among others. The amount I use depends on the types of hot chile selected.

In fact, I add everything according to taste: fresh garlic or freshly ground garlic powder, fresh or dried oregano, and all other seasonings. This will make some purists shudder but I always include tomatoes—my own homegrown whole tomatoes put up in herb-flavored juice—and I always include beans, preferably pink or red. Basic proportions are 1 pound dried beans to each quart of tomatoes and about 1½ pounds coarsely ground lean beef, or half beef and half of my own homemade pork sausage.

Here are two Texas versions, the first from Betty Flemming, who hails from San Antonio. Her recipe includes ground coriander seed and bitter chocolate, not generally found in other versions, and she adds 4 C cooked pinto beans. (Before adding the beans she usually dips out some of the basic mixture to be used for enchilada sauce.) BETTY'S CHILI: In 4 T lard or bacon fat lightly brown 2 C chopped onion, 2 minced cloves of garlic, and 4 pounds finely chopped or coarsely ground chuck. Add 4 to 6 T chili powder, 3 T sugar, 2 squares of bitter chocolate, and 1 T masa harina. Cook and stir until well blended. Add 2 No. 2 cans of tomatoes, 2 C water, 1 T salt, and 1 tsp each ground coriander and cumin seed. Cover and cook on low heat for 1 or 2 hours, stirring occasionally to prevent sticking. Add 4 C cooked pinto beans and cook for another ½ hour, or serve beans on the side.

The second version comes from Taylor Holt, a retired army colonel who was brought up on the Mexican border. He says the basic mixture, before adding chili powder, makes a great sauce for spaghetti, and he either adds beans to the chili "like the cowboys eat it" or serves them on the side. He uses either garlic flakes or garlic-flavored oil (just put peeled cloves of fresh garlic in a cup of peanut oil and keep on hand for flavoring).

First he starts the beans, and to them he adds several things for extra flavor. To 1 pound of soaked, dried pinto or red beans add 1 sliced onion, 1 medium-size can of tomatoes, 2 or 3 ribs of celery with leaves, and salt, pepper, parsley flakes, oregano, and garlic—all to taste. Add 3 C water; cook over low heat until beans are tender but not mushy. When done, fish out celery ribs and add beans to chili or serve on the side.

TAYLOR HOLT'S CHILI: In 2 T bacon grease break up, stir, and lightly brown 1 pound coarsely ground chuck. Add 2 tsp brown sugar, 1 tsp salt, a 6-ounce can of tomato paste, and half the can of water. Cook and stir until well blended. Add, to taste, garlic, minced onion, celery salt, oregano, and parsley flakes. At this stage you have "an excellent spaghetti sauce."

If, instead, you want to make chili, add, to taste, chili powder, ground cumin, garlic, onion salt, and red pepper flakes. Cook for at least 1 hour or so; add beans or serve on side. His recipe ends with: "P.S. I hope this doesn't class me as a Gourmet! My dad called them 'Belly Gods' because they worship their stomachs."

Now for some of the versions that do not include tomatoes. One calls for lean beef cut into 1-inch cubes, olive oil, flour for thickening; chili powder, cumin seeds, oregano, salt, and freshly ground black pepper, all to taste; lots of fresh garlic and beef broth to cover.

Another calls for lean beef cut into ½-inch cubes, browned in lard with chopped onion and garlic. Cover with Chile Colorado Sauce, simmer until meat is tender, add equal amount of cooked frijoles, and simmer for another 30 minutes or so.

To make the CHILE COLORADO SAUCE, cover 6 dried ancho, mulato, or pasilla peppers with 2 C boiling water. Let soak for 1 hour. Lift out peppers with slotted spoon, cut open, remove veins and seeds. In blender combine chile pulp, water in which the peppers soaked, 1 coarsely chopped onion, and 1 clove of garlic. Blend until smooth; add hot chile to taste.

Finally, here is a tomatoless version that doesn't call for any sweet or mild chiles. Remove seeds and veins from

2 long, dried, hot chiles. Cover with 2 C boiling water and let soak for 1 hour. In blender combine soaked chiles, water, and 1 chopped clove of garlic. Blend to make a smooth sauce. Meanwhile cut 2 pounds of lean round steak in ½-inch cubes, dredge with flour, and brown in pork drippings. Add 3 T flour, stir, and mix with meat; when browned add the pint of water-chile-garlic blend. Cover and simmer on low heat for about 2 hours, adding hot water if necessary. When done, add salt to taste.

By now you probably get the idea: chili con carne is good chili just about any way you want to make it to suit your taste. Too, what you serve with it is a matter of choice. Some like it with rice and a selection of garnishes. Me, I'll take mine straight (including the tomatoes and beans), with salad on the side and some type of corn bread—tostados, tortillas, hush puppies, skillet corn bread, corn sticks, or whatever.

Of Machines, Mary Anns, and Good Gifts

Materials and machines are useful servants, but they are degrading masters.
—Donald Duggan, Archbishop of Canterbury

BREATHES there a soul who has not at some time been the degraded slave of some monster machine? If at no other time, at least on Christmas Eve, when "between the dark and the daylight" fiendish materials and machines, in the form of children's toys, have to be assembled with some of the parts missing.

This happens to me all the time; it is the story of my life. I call anything that has moving parts, or parts that have to be moved in order to assemble something, a *machine* and right from the start I know who is master and it ain't me.

When the new stove started buzzing madly and wouldn't stop I first tried pushing and pulling buttons, turning switches on and off, and finally gave up and retreated to the four-poster at the other end of the house, where I couldn't hear it. When Jim got home all he had to do to make it behave was hit it with his fist. When anyone else is around, the washing machine timer doesn't move to "on" until somebody turns it there. When I am here alone it starts clicking and grinding, going through endless cycles of dry runs, and no matter how hard I pull on the reins it won't stop.

When the greenhouse was delivered with instructions saying "easily assembled, requiring nothing more than simple household tools—pliers and screwdriver," I knew *that* was a base lie and called in a couple of competent workmen at the start. Even they, using drills, sprockets, wrenches, ratchets, and whatever all those things are, couldn't get the framework put together. Finally we laid out the whole thing on the two acres of lawn between the house and the pond, like a giant erector set, and I checked every one of the 79,563 items on the invoice, including all the nuts and bolts, and we found that the leg bone that connected the thigh bone to the ankle bone was missing. The manufacturer assured me this had never happened before. Naturally not. I hadn't bought a greenhouse before.

Any time Jim is going to be away for a few days, everything mechanical on the place passes the word along, and he no sooner turns onto the road at the end of our lane than the water pump stops pumping, the sump pump starts sumping, and all hell breaks loose up here at the house. Then, when I decide to just flee the scene, the car won't start.

Thus it was with considerable trepidation and after a lot of thought I decided to buy my Tricer (otherwise known as a food processor). I give a lot of thought before buying any new piece of kitchen equipment. For instance, my covered chicken fryer had already lost its handle and its knob before I got it thirty-five years ago, since then it has developed a decided bulge in its bottom, but I am still *thinking* about buying a new one. Then there was the distinct possibility that any machine that could crush, cut, slice, shred, grate, and "grind exceeding fine" just about anything you put in it, faster than tongue could tell, might also grab stray parts of me and start shredding.

But finally I paid my money and took my chances and I must say it is the greatest thing to come into the kitchen since a full-time cook and kitchen maid went out. It comes as close as anything can to being foolproof. I can manage to stitch my own thumb while using the sewing machine, but I don't see how it would be possible, even for me, to get fingers down in the Tricer blades. The machine can't be activated until the top is in place, and extending above the top is a tube through which food has to be inserted. If you had fingers nine inches long you might be able to reach those blades; otherwise, no way.

There are a few things it won't do as well as might be done by another method, such as beat egg whites or cut vegetables into uniform julienne strips or dice, but the things it will do are almost incredible to watch and the time it saves is equally unbelievable—and it couldn't be easier to clean.

One morning recently, in quick succession, I grated four kinds of cheese—Romano, Parmesan, Gruyère, and sharp yellow. Next I grated fine crumbs for casserole toppings, soft bread crumbs, cracker crumbs, and all of the making for the turkey dressing. Each of these jobs was done in seconds. In less than half an hour everything was bagged up and in the freezer. Another morning I made the dough for a couple of pies, two kinds of cocktail wafers, and three kinds of cookies, everything from nut grinding to final mixing done in a matter of a few minutes. Still another day I made some paté, two kinds of dip, stuffing for celery, and a blue cheese dressing for salads. When I organize jobs like this, the Tricer only has to be washed once, at the end of a session, but it is so easy to clean I don't hesitate to use it for a single chore such as shredding cabbage for slaw or grating potatoes for pancakes.

Another kitchen purchase this year was *The Cooks'*

Catalogue. It didn't list a number of things I was looking for and told me more than I care to know about some others, but it was worth the price because it answered a question that had been fretting me for some time. A while back a reader had asked me what a Mary Ann cup was. The name rang a bell but there was no answer. (Is there anything more frustrating than having the feeling you *know* something but can't remember what it is?) I went through all my collection of cookbooks and couldn't find a clue, consulted all the home economists in the county and none of them had ever heard of it, and then started asking everyone I knew and several people I don't know all that well. No one knew for sure and suggestions ranged all the way from a punch, or drink, to a chamber pot.

Then came *The Cooks' Catalogue*, with a picture of a Mary Ann pan, and did I ever feel like an idiot. A Mary Ann is a large or individual-size cake with a shallow cup or depression in the top. We see them all the time, at every supermarket, usually suggested for serving filled with strawberries. Now, everywhere I look I see Mary Anns—all of them with the name right there in large print on the package—and feel like a fool all over again.

Now if they had just asked me about MADELEINES. I make them so often I couldn't forget them, at least I hope not. To my way of thinking, these shell-shaped little cakes are perfect to serve with tea; feather light in texture, fragrant with fresh lemon, and not too sweet. Over the years I've tried numerous recipes for them but the one I like best starts with 4 egg yolks, beaten at high speed with 1½ C sugar, 1¼ C melted butter, and 1 T lemon juice until smooth and thick. Turn down speed and blend in 2⅓ C sifted flour, continue beating, and add the 4 egg whites, one at a time. (The egg whites are not beaten before adding them to the batter.) When the batter is smooth, drop by teaspoon into Madeleine forms that have been buttered and dusted with flour or sprayed with a nonstick preparation. Bake about 25 minutes at 325°. When done, tip out cakes, shell side up, and sprinkle with sifted confectioner's sugar.

Of Machines, Mary Anns, and Good Gifts / 215

A Christmas gift that made a real hit with me is a charlotte mold. Lacking the proper mold has never stopped me from making a charlotte, but it will be more fun with this charming little one. But that must wait until after the holidays are over and recovered from. Right now I plan to take a sabbatical from KP duty for a few days, "set a spell" or even put my feet up, and read some of the gift books, To Me from Me and From Me to Me. One of them is Eliot Porter's *Birds of North America*. What a beautiful book this is! I have never seen such color photographs of birds. I don't suppose there will ever be a complete book of birds done like this—the few species included represent over thirty years' work—but what a magnificent thing it would be.

Another of the gift books is *An Almanac of Words at Play* by Willard R. Espy. It can be enjoyed in solitude, but it is the sort of book that should be read aloud, to share the fun.

A real find was the recently reprinted *Journal of Nicholas Cresswell*. Nicholas Cresswell left England for America in 1774 and returned in 1777, keeping a diary throughout the time he was in this country. The whole thing is fascinating, some of the more amusing entries being made while he was in Loudoun County—since his candid account of all the carrying-on gives such a different picture from the staid and sober records on the same people in the local historical archives.

On December 31, 1775, Cresswell wrote, "This is the last day of the year 1775, which I have spent but very indifferently. In short I have done nothing, but wore out my clothes and constitution." Well, I can sympathize. At the end of any year I feel as if I have "wore out my clothes and constitution," but I hope I haven't spent a day, much less than a year, indifferently.

I don't spend much time looking back, except to remember the happy times. Before one year ends, another has begun. Just ten days ago we had the shortest day in the year, which means they're already getting longer.

December

Before we know it, it will be time to order seeds, plan, and plant for another season. Growing things are already stirring underground, ready to start their journey up to the air and sun.

On Hogmanay, or New Year's Eve, Mother always had us eat herring, to make sure we would have a healthy, happy, prosperous year to come. (Some years I thought the spell hadn't been working—but who knows, things might have been much worse if we hadn't eaten the herring.)

Whatever your customs are, remember a saying from the Scots—a year must begin happily to end happily—so be *happy,* and have a Guid New Year—and the taste of goodness, every day, every year.

Index

Albondigas, 40
Apple(s):
  Bread, 162
  Butter, 163
  Candy, 163
  Cider Ice, 204
  Cider, Mulled, 205
  Cider Snow, 204
  Crisp, 162–63
  Fried, 160
  Jelly, 163
  Lemon Jellied, 201–2
  Muffins, 162
  Pie, 161
  Rosy, 161
  Struggle, 162
Applesauce, 160
  Cake, 160–61
  canning and freezing, 160
  Pudding, 161
Apricot Candy, 203
Artichokes, Jerusalem:
  Au Gratin, 154
  Baked, 155
  Boiled, 154
  in cream sauce, 154
  Fried (fritters), 154
  Girasole Salad, 154
  in Oriental dishes, 154
  Palestine Soup, 154
  pickle and relishes, 155–56
  preparing tubers, 153–54
  pureed, 154
  sautéed, 155
  in salad, 154
Asparagus (fresh), preparing and cooking methods, 65–66
Aspic, Tomato, 192

Baking powder:
  biscuits, 44
  types and substitutes, 14
Batty Cakes, cornmeal, 186

Bean Soup with Ham, 34, 60
Beans:
  Baked, 63
  Green (in pickle), 124
  and Lamb Casserole, 34
  Leather Britches, 63
  Pinto or Red Chili, 209–10
Beaten Biscuits, 75
Beets, cooked with tops, 112
Benne seed:
  Drop Cookies, 148
  other suggested uses, 148
  Wafers, 148
Betty's Chili, 209
Beverages:
  Apple Cider Snow, 204
  Blackberry Cordial, 120
  Coffee Essence, 30–31
  Dandelion Wine, 103
  Eggnog, 204
  Mulled Cider, 205
Biscuit-wrapped Links or Franks, 45
Biscuits:
  Baking Powder, 44
  Beaten, 75
  Buttermilk, 44
  Cheese, 45
  Cream, sweet or sour, 45
  Pinwheel, 45
  Sweet Potato, 26–27
Bishop's Cake, 182
Bisque, Tomato, 40
Black Walnut:
  Bread, 181
  Divine Divinity, 202
  Spicy Prune Cake, 181
Blackberry:
  Cobbler, 118
  Cordial, 120
  Jam, 119
  Jam Cake, 119
  Jelly, 120
  Pudding, 119

Blackberry (cont.):
  Roly-Poly, 118
  Slump, 118
  Syrup, 120
Bluefish, Broiled, 172
Bourbon Sauce, 188
Braised Venison, 176
Bread:
  Dressing Balls, 191
  Pudding, Chocolate, 24
Bread and Butter Pickles, 138
Breadmaking, 81
Breads (loaf):
  Apple, 162
  Black Walnut, 181
  Brown, 63
  Chewy Rye, 83
  Corn-Wheat, 87
  Cottage Loaf, 59
  French, 85
  household loaves, 85–86
  Persimmon, 170
  Quick Crusty, 82
  Sourdough, 83–84
  Sourdough Rye, 83
  Zuke-Bran, 129
Broiled Bluefish, 172
Brown Bread, 63
Buttermilk Biscuits, 44
Buttermilk Custard Pie, 171

Cabbage salad, 40
Cake:
  Applesauce, 160–61
  Bishop's, 182
  Blackberry Jam, 119
  Daisy, 46
  Devil's Food, 56
  Hickory Nut, 179
  Orange Frost, 47
  Persimmon, 170
  Spicy Prune, 181
  Whipped Cream, 20
  Wild Rose, 46
Candied Sweet Potatoes, 29
Candied Tomatoes, 76
Candy and Confections:
  Apple, 163
  Apricot, 203
  Divine Divinity, 202
  Sugared Popcorn, 202
  White Pralines, 202
Carrots, Smothered, 192
Casseroles:
  Bean and Lamb, 34
  Dutch Country, 50
  Easter Egg, 77
  Mixed Vegetable, 42
  Oyster and Dressing, 191–92
  Pasta Shells and Cheese, 149
  Summer Garden, 127
  Sweet 'Tater and Sausage, 28
  Tomato-Macaroni, 141
  vegetable-meat combinations, 141
Cauliflower Custard, 76
Cheese:
  Biscuits, 45
  and Grits Soufflé, 188
  Sauce with Eggs, 77
  Strada, 66
Chewy Rye Bread, 83
Chile Colorado Sauce, 210
Chili con Carne, 207
  Betty's, 209
  hot pepper sauce, 210–11
  Monday's version, 19
  Taylor Holt's, 210
Chili Powder, 208
Chili Sauce, Tomato, 139
Chips, Sweet Potato, 30
Chocolate:
  Bread Pudding, 24
  Cookies, 199
  Devil's Food Cake, 56
Chowder, 61

Chutney:
  Fresh Mango or Peach, 116
  Mango-Peach, 135
Cobbler, Blackberry, 118
Conserve, Damson Plum, 146
Coffee Maker, Toddy, 30–31
Cookie:
  cutters and decorating, 195–96
  icing and glaze, 197
Cookies and small cakes, 194
  Benne Seed Drops, 148
  Benne Wafers, 148
  Dreams, 199
  Ginger, 196
  Hickory Nut, 179–80
  Lemon Wafers, 200–201
  Madeleines, 214
  Meringue Kisses, 201
  Moravian Christmas, 198–99
  Oat Crisps, 199
  Peppernuts, Brown, 197
  Peppernuts, White, 198
  Rolled Wafers, 200
  Sand Bars, 199
  Southern Crisps, 200
  Super Chocolate, 199
Cordial, Blackberry, 120
Corn Pudding, Dried, 76
Corn-Wheat Bread, 87
Corn Bread:
  Dressing, 191
  Oak Hill, 186
  Skillet, 186
  toasted, 187
Corncob Syrup, 188
Cornmeal:
  Batty Cakes, 186
  Crisps, 187
  Hush Puppies, 19, 59
  Muffins, 186
  Mush, 185
  Mush, Fried, 185
  Pone, 187

Spoon Bread, everyday, 187
Spoon Bread, Sarah's, 173
Sticks, 186
types, 14
Cottage Loaf, 59
Crab-Stuffed Zucchini, 128
Cream Biscuits, 45
Creamy Pumpkin Soup, 166
Creasies (cress), cooked and in
  salad, 88–89
Crisps, Corn, 187
Crunchy Buttons, 22
  Peanutty, 22
  Nutty-Cheese, 22
  Rosemary, 22
Crust, Crunchy, 22
Cumberland Sauce, 177
Curried Eggs, 77
Custard:
  Cauliflower, 76
  Hickory Nut, 179
  Zucchini, 128
Cymlins, see Squash, white

Daisy Cake, 46
Damson Plum Conserve, 146
Dandelion:
  cooked greens, 80
  Homely Sallet, 79
  Tea, 78
  Wine, 79
Desserts:
  Apple Cider Ice, 204
  Apple Crisp, 162
  Applesauce, Sherbet, 160, with
    whipped cream, 160
  Apple Struggle, 162
  Meringue Tart, 67
  peaches, frozen, 42
  Sabayon, 20
Deviled Eggs, 77
Devil's Food Cake, 56
Divine Divinity, 202

Index /219

Index

Dorothy's Onion Relish, 137
Dressing, corn bread, 191
Dutch Country Casserole, 50

Easter Egg Casserole, 77
Eggnog, 204
Eggplant, 127
Eggs:
  in Cheese Sauce, 77
  Curried, 77
  Deviled, 77
  Easter Casserole, 77
  Omelet, 55
  in Patty Shells, 77
  in Snow, 41
El Fatso Pecan Pie, 182
Elderflower:
  Fritters, 103
  Tea, 103
  Vinegar, 103
  Wine, 103
Empanadas, Pumpkin, 167
English Muffins, sourdough, 84

Fish:
  Broiled Bluefish, 172
  chowder, 61
Food Processor, see Tricer
Franks:
  in biscuit strips, 45
  in hot potato salad, 23
Freezing:
  Applesauce, 160
  Biscuits, 45
  Fried Tomatoes, 139
  Nuts, 182
  Peaches, 42
  Ratatouille, 127
  Squash, 129
  Stuffed Peppers, 171–72
  Sweet Potatoes, 26
  Tomatoes, 143–44
  Vegetable casseroles, 42

Vegetables, 129
French Bread, 85
Fried Tomatoes, 139
Fritters:
  Elderflower, 103
  Fried Jerusalem 'Chokes, 154
Fruit:
  in Meringue Tart, 67
  Salad, 19
Fudge (Divine Divinity), 202
Fyshe Pottage, 61

Game:
  marinades, 176
  methods for cooking rabbit and venison, 176–77
  plucking waterfowl, 178
  roasting goose, 177
  Vine-wrapped Quail, 177
  Wild Duck, 177–78
Garlic-Herb Pickles, 124
Garlic oil, 209
Gazpacho, 141
Ginger Cookies, 196
Girasole Salad, 154
Gravy:
  Fried Tomato, 139
  Red-Eye, 188
Green-Tomato Relish, 136
Grits, to cook, 188
  Leftover, suggestions, 188
  Soufflé with Cheese, 188

Ham:
  in Bean Soup, 34, 60
  Maryland Stuffed, 74
  in Vegetable Soup, 59
Hasenpfeffer, 177
Herb-Flavored Tomato Juice, 142
Hickory Nut:
  Cake, 179
  Cookies, 179
  Custard, 179

Higdon Salad, 136–37
Hollandaise Sauce, made in Tricer, 66
Homely Sallet, 79
Hot Potato-Frank Salad, 23
Household Loaf, 85–86
Hush Puppies:
  plain, 19
  with onion, 59

Jam, Blackberry, 119
Jelly:
  Apple, 163
  Blackberry, 120
  Mint, 163
  Scented Geranium, 163
Jerusalem Artichoke Pickles, 155–56

Laitue Suedoise, 40
Lamb and Bean Casserole, 34
Lemon Jellied Apples, 201–2
Lemon Sauce, 23
Lemon Wafers, 200–201
Lentil Soup, 59
Lib's Artichoke Pickle, 155–56

Macaroni-Tomato Casserole, 141
Madeleines, 214
Mango:
  Fresh Chutney, 166
  and Peach Chutney, 135
Marinades for meat and game, 176
Meat and vegetable combinations for soup, 58–59
Meatballs for soup, 41
Meringue Kisses, 201
Meringue Tart, 67
Mittie's Artichoke Pickle, 156
Mixed Vegetable Soup, 58
Moravian Christmas Cookies, 198–99

Muffins:
  Apple, 162
  Cornmeal, 186
  English, sourdough, 84
Mulled Cider, 205
Mush, Cornmeal, 185

Nellie's Pudding, 23
Nutty-Cheese Buttons, 22

Oak Hill Corn Bread, 186
Oat Crisps, 199
Omelet, French, 55
Omelet Sauce, 56
Onions:
  creamed, 192
  Dorothy's Relish, 137
  and garlic (wild), 89
Orange Frost Cake, 47
Oyster-Dressing Casserole, 191–92

Palestine Soup, 154
Pancakes, cornmeal, 186
Parsnips, Peppy, 24
Pasta Shells and Cheese, 149
Pattypans, see Squash, white
Pawpaws, to ripen, 169
Pea Soup, 59
Peach(es):
  freezing, 42
  Fresh Chutney, 116
  and Mango Chutney, 135
  Piquant, 42
  Salad, 42
Peanutty Buttons, 22
Pecan:
  El Fatso Pie, 182
  Sand Bars, 199
  Southern Crisps, 200
  White Pralines, 202
Peppernuts, 197–98
Peppers, Stuffed, 28, 171–72

Persimmon:
  Bread, 170
  Cake, 170
  Pudding, 170
Pickles:
  Bread and Butter, 138
  Garlic-Herb, 124
  general hints and tips, 133
  Jerusalem Artichoke, 155–56
  Sugar-Free, 138
  Super Sweet Chips, 134
  Watermelon, 135
Pie:
  Apple, 161
  Buttermilk Custard, 171
  Pumpkin, 193
  Sweet Potato, 30
Pie Crust:
  paste method, 161
  whole wheat (Crunchy), 22
Pinwheel Biscuits, 45
Plum:
  Conserve, Damson, 146
  Sauce, 51
Pone:
  Corn, 187
  Sweet Potato, 27
Popcorn, Sugared, 202
Pork:
  Roast, 29
  see also Sausage
Possum and Sweet 'Taters, 29
Potato, sweet, *see* Sweet Potato
Potato-Frank Salad, 23
Pot Herbs, 71–72, 88
Pralines, White, 202
Prune Cake, 181
Pudding:
  Applesauce, 161
  Blackberry, 119
  Chocolate Bread, 24
  Dried Corn, 76
  Nellie's, 23

Persimmon, 170
  sauce for, 171
  Sweet Potato, 27
  Yellow Squash, 124
Puffs, Sweet Potato, 28
Pumpkin:
  Butter, 167
  Creamy Soup, 166
  Empanadas, 167
  Pie, 193
  seeds, to roast, 166

Quail, Vine-Wrapped, 177
Quick Crusty Bread, 82

Ratatouille, 127
Red-Eye Gravy, 188
Relish:
  Green-Tomato, 136
  Higdon Salad, 136–37
  Jerusalem Artichoke, 155
  Onion, Dorothy's, 137
  Red-Tomato, 136
Rolled Wafers, 200
Roly-Poly, Blackberry, 118
Rose water, 14
Rosemary Buttons, 22
Rosy Apple Salad, 161
Rye Bread, Chewy, 83

Sabayon, 20
Saccharine Pickles, 138
Saftborn (steam juicer), 119–20
Salad:
  Cabbage, 40
  Fruit, 19
  Gazpacho, 141
  Girasole, 154
  Homely Sallet, 79
  Hot Potato-Frank, 23
  Peach, 42
  Rosy Apple, 161
  Tomato Aspic, 192

Index /223

Salsa, 41
Sand Bars, 199
Sandwiches:
  Baked Bean, 63
  Tomato, Broiled or Grilled, 140
Sauce:
  Chili, 139
  Hollandaise (Tricer), 66
  Mexican Salsa, 41
  Omelet, 56
  Ratatouille, 127
  Taylor Holt's Spaghetti, 210
Sauces, Sweet:
  Bourbon, 188
  Cumberland, 177
  Lemon, 23
  Plum, 51
  Simple Pudding, 171
Sausage (Pork):
  making and freezing, 146–47
  in biscuit strips, 45
  in Stuffed Peppers, 28
  in Summer Casserole, 128
  in Sweet Potato Casserole, 28
Seeds:
  edible, 148–49
  pumpkin, to roast, 166
Senate Bean Soup, 60
Sesame, see Benne
Sherbet, Tomato, 144
Simple Pudding Sauce, 171
Skillet Corn Bread, 186
Slump, Blackberry, 118
Soup:
  Albondigas, 40
  Bean with Ham, 34, 60–61
  Creamy Pumpkin, 166
  Fyshe Pottage, 61
  Lentil, 59
  Mixed Vegetable and variations, 58
  Palestine, 154

Split Pea, 59
Squash, 125
Tomato Bisque, 40
Vegetable-Cream, 125
Soup and stock pot, 61
Sourdough:
  Bread, 84
  English Muffins, 84
  regular starter, 84
  rye starter, 83
Southern Candied Tomatoes, 76
Southern Crisps, 200
Spaghetti Sauce, Taylor Holt's, 210
Special equipment:
  Saftborn (steam juicer), 119–20
  stock pot, 61
  Toddy Coffee Maker, 30–31
  Tricer (Food Processor), 66, 212
Spicy Prune Cake, 181
Split Pea Soup, 59
Spoon Bread:
  everyday, 187
  Sarah's, 173
Squash:
  Blossoms, Fried, 123
  freezing, 129
  Garlic-Herb Pickle, 124
  Steamed, 124
Squash, green (zucchini and others), 126
  Casserole, 127
  Custard, 128
  Masako's Crab-Stuffed, 128
  Ratatouille, 127
  Sautéed, 126
  Zuke-Bran Bread, 129
Squash, white (cymlins):
  Deep-Fried, 125
  Stewed, 125
  Stuffed, 126

Index

Squash, yellow:
  Pudding, 124
  Soup, 125
  Supreme, 124
Sticks, Corn, 186
Stuffed Ham, 74
Stuffed Peppers, 28, 171–72
Stuffed Tomatoes, 140
Stuffing, see Dressing
Strada, 66
Strudel, Apple, see Apple Struggle
Sub Gum, Turkey, 50
Sugar-Free Pickles, 138
Summer Garden Casserole, 127
Super Sweet Chips, 134
Sweet Potato(es):
  Biscuits, 26–27
  Candied, 29
  Casserole (with sausage), 28
  Chips, 30
  Flambé, 31
  Mashed, 26
  Nests, 29
  Pie, 30
  Pone, 27
  Pudding, 27
  Puffs, 28
  Roast (with pork or possum), 28–29.
  Stuffed Peppers, 28
Syrup:
  Blackberry, 120
  Corncob, 188

'Tater-Stuffed Peppers, 28
Taylor Holt's Chili, 210
Taylor Holt's Spaghetti Sauce, 210
Toasted Corn Bread, 187
Tomato(es):
  Aspic, 192
  Bisque, 40
  Chili Sauce, 139

freezing, 143
freezing for sherbet, 144
Fried, 139
fried before freezing, 140
Gravy, 140
Green, Garlic-Herb Pickle, 124
and Herb Juice, 142
home canning, 142
and Macaroni Casserole, 141
Relish, Green, 136
Relish, Red, 136
sandwiches, hot, 140
Southern Candied, 76
Stuffed, 140
Tricer, 66, 212
Turkey: Roast, 190, in bag, 191
  Stuffing, 191
  Sub Gum, 50

Upland cress, see Creasies

Vegetable Casserole, 42
Vegetable Cream Soup, 125
Venison, Braised, 176
Vine-Wrapped Quail, 177

Watermelon Pickle, 135
Wheat germ:
  for casserole toppings, 149
  in Cottage Loaf, 59
  Wafers, see Crunchy Buttons
Whipped Cream Cake, 20
White Pralines, 202
Wild garlic and onion, 89
Wild Rose Cake, 46
Winter cress, see Creasies

Yams Flambé, 31
Yeast used in recipes, 81

Zucchini, see Squash, green
Zuke-Bran Bread, 129